To Walk with Lions

7 *Spiritual Principles I Learned from Living with Lions*

GARETH PATTERSON

Seastone

BERKELEY, CALIFORNIA

Published by: Seastone, an imprint of Ulysses Press
P.O. Box 3440
Berkeley, CA 94703
www.ulyssespress.com

First published in the United Kingdom by Rider, an imprint of Ebury Press, Random House

Library of Congress Control Number: 2001094718
ISBN: 1-56975-278-8

Printed in Canada by Transcontinental Printing

10 9 8 7 6 5 4 3 2 1

Editor: Richard Harris
Editorial and production staff: Claire Chun, Lily Chou,
    Marin Van Young
Design: Leslie Henriques and Sarah Levin
Cover Photography: Mark Newman/Superstock

Distributed in the United States by Publishers Group West
and in Canada by Raincoast Books

To the memory of my mother Joyce,
who, with her great love of nature, understood that the
glory and power of God "lies hidden in a flower."

Table of Contents

Acknowledgements

With much gratitude to: Judith Kendra of Rider Books; my agent Tony Peake of Peake Associates; my editor Susan Lascelles; Fransje van Riel, my loving partner.

The author would like to thank the following for permission to use copyright material:

Jonathan Cape for material from Sue McCarthy's and Jeffrey Masson's *When Elephants Weep* (1994); Hodder & Stoughton for material for Alan F. Alford's *The Phoenix Solution* (1998); Penguin Books for material from David Maybury-Lewis' *Millennium* (1992) and for material from Kate Turkington's *There's More to Life than Surface* (1998); Piatkus Publishers Ltd. for material from Owen Burnham's *African Wisdom* (2000); Tim Stoffel for material from his *The Lion of Judah and the King of Pride Rock*; Struik Publishers for material from Credo Mutwa's *Isilwane* (1996); Swan Hill Press for material from Brian Jackman's *Roaring at Dawn* (1995); Thames & Hudson for material from Kenneth Clarke's *Animals and Men* (1977); University of South Africa Press for material from S. A. Thorpe's *African Traditional Religions* (1991); and Virgin Publishing for material from Sue Carpenter's *Past Lives* (1995).

Every effort has been made to trace all copyright holders but if any have been inadvertently overlooked, the publishers will be pleased to make the necessary arrangement at the first opportunity.

Preface

We live in a world that prides itself on its modernity, yet
is hungry for wholeness, hungry for meaning. At the same
time it is a world that marginalizes those very impulses
that might fill the void. The pilgrimage to the divine, the
openness that transcends ordinary experience, the very
idea of feeling at one with the Universe, these are
impulses which we tolerate at the fringes, where they are
held at bay by our indifference. The irony is that, after
excluding the mystical tradition from our cultural main-
stream and claiming to find it irrelevant to our concerns,
so many of us feel empty without it.

DAVID MAYBURY-LEWIS—*Millennium*[1]

I have lived as a man among lions and I have lived as a "lion man" among modern people. Living in these two worlds, I have seen "wholeness" in lions and I have seen "disconnectedness" in people.

From this experience I have sensed that many in the modern world yearn for meaning in their lives. Consciously or unconsciously, openly or secretly, there is a yearning for wholeness—a wholeness that has become eroded in Western structured society. Separated from nature, we have become separated from what we yearn for. We have become separated from our very essence.

To Walk with Lions takes you on a mystical journey toward the rediscovery of the nature of God and the rediscovery of the essential reverence of that nature. Man, nature and God have become separated in the modern era, leaving us spiritually and environmentally impoverished. There is, though, just enough time to begin to repair the damage done to nature and ourselves. When we see ourselves as a part of the natural world, destruction of the natural world can be recognized only as self-destruction. By acknowledging this fact, we can begin to heal ourselves and the natural world. There is an enormous need for us to understand that in nature "her ultimate message is the friendship of God. Secure in that friendship we cannot be afraid."[2]

To Walk with Lions is also about releasing oneself from the prison of loneliness of spirit, to feel a part of all around one (and to feel the nature within). With this we can begin to heal nature around us and within us.

CHAPTER 1

A Golden Moment

Beauty will come in the dawn
And beauty will come with the sunlight
Beauty will come to us from everywhere
Where the heaven ends, where the sky ends,
Beauty will surround us. We walk in beauty.

BILLY YELLOW, Navajo medicine man[3]

Why did early man, when he expressed himself in rock
engravings, choose animals as emblems of his aspirations?
Why have highly cultured races like the Egyptians and
Assyrians used animals as symbols for their Gods...? Why
are we so deeply moved by tragedies involving our pets?
Why are the first toys given to our children representa-
tives of animals? ... Do we need more proof that we need
animals more than they need us—that they can give us
something which we cannot give ourselves?

JOY ADAMSON—*Pippa's Challenge*[4]

*F*or years in Africa I fought poaching, trophy hunting, the trade in lions and loss of habitat—all fueled by human greed. The problems affecting the lion and wildlife are a portion of the ill health humans inflict upon the earth (and ultimately, ourselves). Recently I began to understand that unless we address the health of the earth, collectively and holistically, the symptoms of our own inner health will persist and will worsen. The health of the planet and our own inner health are one.

The earth is our mother and, as I write, I can feel so deeply the pain we inflict on her. With every single tree felled, with every particle of poison we release into the air and pour into the soil, with every death of an animal by the hand of man and in the name of "sport," and with the callous leveling of land and places once natural to make way for so-called development in the name of "progress," the earth is wounded again and again. We are killing our mother.

The following two passages sum up the crisis we have created—a crisis of only our own making but whose effects threaten all life:

Rainforests are felled at the rate of 15 million hectares [37 million acres] every year—an area three times the

size of Denmark. The oceans are polluted and over-
fished, coral reefs are dying in every region of the
globe. The earth's protective ozone layer is weakened,
and global warming could bring rising seas and
climatic change. All these human-induced changes
threaten us and every other species on earth. Today
we are living through the greatest mass extinction of
species since the end of the dinosaurs.[5]

There has never been a bigger crisis than the one
we now face. And we are the last generation that can
pull us out of it. We must act because this is the only
home we have. It's a matter of survival.[6]

Our harm of ourselves, our outer destruction and self-
destruction, can be viewed as a modern disease. Humankind is
a product of nature and throughout almost our entire evolution-
ary history on earth we lived in nature, a part of nature. But in
these strange, often frightening modern times it is as if humans
have become unnatural, have become like some alien parasites
that feed so relentlessly upon their host that ultimately they will
die, having consumed totally what their own survival was dependent upon.

In these modern times we have acted as though all things
natural were only there to serve us and were infinite, inexhaust-
ible. Separate from God and nature we destroyed, consumed
and feasted. The more we took from the earth the more spiritually
impoverished we became. And as individuals we became alone
and isolated, surrounded and choked in the crowds of our kind.
Disconnected from the whole, we acted as though we were above
all other life. The reality is that in the modern age, we tragically
became nakedly alone and separate from divine nature.

The following passages hauntingly describe what has happened in these modern times.

Sacred beauty has been destroyed and defiled ... Once
again the cult of separation has claimed its victims

and the loss of course is ours. Wisdom has been reduced to orthodoxy, holistic spirituality has become narrow religious observance. The priestesses have become invisible.[7]

It is a sad truth that since the Age of Enlightenment—the intellectual movement of the eighteenth century which generated so much supposed wisdom and understanding—the western path has led most of its followers to anything but enlightenment. Sooner or later most people come to realize that materialism does not bring happiness. But by that time, their spiritual lives represent such a void that it is difficult to know which way to turn for inner fulfillment.[8]

Nothing is meant to be separate from the whole. Separation equals loneliness of spirit and with loneliness of spirit comes disconnection. And when people are disconnected they become like the caged lion in a zoo. Though his food and shelter are provided, because he is separated from his kind and his natural habitat the zoo lion is lost to the whole, a facsimile of his kind. Because he cannot connect, something dies within.

The caged zoo lion is groundless, alone. Daily he walks the unnatural path to nowhere, endlessly pacing up and down, up and down, going nowhere. He is lost to the whole.

Are we now, in this modern age, becoming like the caged zoo lion? Are we now, individuals in the modern age, feeling that we too are walking the path to nowhere? Are we becoming (or have we already become) mentally and physically isolated from the natural whole?

With these questions in mind I wrote this book, which is about transformation and spiritual liberty. It is about releasing ourselves from the cage that we have created around us, isolating us, and it is about what we can learn from the lion to enrich our lives.

In my life I have walked many paths, some of which led to beautiful light while others led me into great darkness.

One morning, about ten years ago, my path led me into great golden light. That day I was walking with a lion. This is what happened.

My golden moment happened as I stood next to a young male lion called Batian in the midst of the African bush. Batian was then of an age when he would soon enter adulthood. The young prince was to become a king. He was maturing and I suspected that he had begun calling for the first time the dramatic song of a territorial lion, the leonine song that has been interpreted by some as meaning:

> Whose land is this ...? Whose land is this ...? It is
> mine. It is mine. It is mine ...

Suddenly, as I stood beside Batian, at the start of a new day, he began to call, roaring to the dawn. My right hand was resting lightly on his flank. Batian's calls reverberated through the valley we were in, to the highest hills arid within the ground we stood upon. The trees seemed to vibrate with his mighty song. Time stopped and through his calls I felt I was a part of everything around me. A portion of my soul was enriched by a beautiful energy that I can only describe as the "connection energy of the earth." I was the lion, and the lion was me. I was the sky, I was the birds, I was every leaf on every tree, I was every grain of sand in every dry streambed, I was the earth and the earth was me. I belonged, and I was free.

Those were moments of wonder. And it was then that the true meaning of the lion's song crystallized within me. Lions call to the world—

> I am the land, the land is me,
> I belong, I belong, I belong....

Like us, lions are social beings. Every lion in the pride has a purpose, and to me a lion's pride is the ultimate expression of the traditional African philosophy called "Ubuntu." Ubuntu is

ship of all life principles were horrified by the destruction caused by the European settlers. Chief Luther Standing Bear of the Lakota said, "Forests were mowed down, the buffalo exterminated, the beaver driven to extinction ... The white man has come to be the symbol of extinction for all things natural in this continent."

"What," Chief Seattle asked in 1854, "what is man without the beasts? If all the beasts were gone, man would die from a great loneliness of spirit. For whatever happens to the beasts soon happens to man. All things are connected."

And Chief Seattle could have been speaking for all indigenous peoples colonized worldwide in the past (and for the wild lands and their wildlife) when he said:

> We know that the White man does not understand our ways. One portion of land is the same to him as the next, for he is a stranger who comes in the night and takes from the land whatever he needs. The earth is not his brother, but his enemy, and when he conquers it, he moves on. He leaves his father's grave behind and does not care. His fathers' graves and his children's birthright are forgotten. He treats his mother the earth, and his brother the sky, as things to be bought, plundered, sold like sheep and bright beads. His appetite will devour the earth and leave behind only desert.[13]

In Africa, the land, its people and wildlife were also cursed by the European settlers armed with their "dominion over" attitude. On both sides of the Atlantic, the settlers brought to the land an obsessive need to try to subdue nature, coupled with disconnectedness and insensitivity. The white man's religious beliefs (unlike the indigenous peoples' beliefs) did not allow him to feel a part of the environment, but rather apart from it, seeing it as something from which to extract what he perceived as "wealth" to be used for selfish reasons. There was none of the reciprocity characteristic of tribal societies toward nature. The knowledge

of the interconnectedness of man and nature had become lost
to the white man.

The West African shaman and scholar Malidoma Patrice Somé
once wrote: "As part of the healing that we all deserve and all
need, the natural world calls us ... shedding our own tears of
grief for the violence done to nature and for the alienation and
losses we have experienced in our lives will open the doors to
healing ..."[14] Sorrow can then be replaced by joy, joy that we can,
if we wish to, feel again as a part of all around us. And what a joy
this truly is. It is a loving joy, a joy that consists of feeling free
and identifying yourself, your very soul in all things of beauty
in nature. Who can really persecute you today for loving the
earth, for loving yourself, for understanding that individuals are
strands of the web of life, with us all having a purpose?

Instead of allowing feelings of groundlessness to pervade us,
we can reach out again and reconnect. By embracing a theology
of the earth we are creating a positive antithesis to the environmental values, or rather lack of values, which have existed for
so long. It is the turning point. The path of reconnection lies in
front of us.

How does one begin to reconnect? How does one reconnect if one lives in a city? I talk more about this in Chapter 4.
But before then, I would like to offer the following reconnection
exercise as a first step in the overall process.

Firstly, you do not have to be standing next to a lion roaring at the dawn to experience and access the earth's connection
energy! In all likelihood you have already felt the connection
energy in varying degrees, perhaps by seeing a beautiful sunset,
or the sun on autumn leaves, or the beauty of snowflakes falling
from the sky. We can feel the connection with the earth almost
anywhere, for we exist on the divine—we are touching it every
day. Every step we take connects us to mother earth. We are a
part of it and it surrounds us. We breathe it.

Each day, we all need to remind ourselves:

You are never lost or alone so long as you can claim
kinship with everything that is. You are no more alone
than the river is alone or the mountains are alone or
anything in the Universe, for you are a part of the
whole ... Every day you can come out and meet yourself in the sky's reflection, or the dew lying on flowers'
petals or any other natural thing. Renew yourself in
these things, identify yourself with them....[15]

The following basic meditation exercise is particularly for those
who live in busy towns or cities. Try to do this exercise once each day.
It takes a little time, but you deserve to give yourself a little time each
day. It will become easier with practice.

1. If you cannot surround yourself with natural sounds and
   sights (for example a field or a park) retreat to your
   sanctuary at home—which is probably your bedroom.

2. If possible, play a relaxation tape or CD and sit (either on
   your bed or on the floor) in the position you feel most
   comfortable in.

3. Drop your shoulders and begin to relax. Breathe in slowly
   and steadily, hold your breath for two seconds, then
   breathe out (a little more deeply than normal). Try to
   breathe like this throughout this exercise.

4. Let tension drain away from you, first from your head,
   then from your shoulders and downward. Feel tension
   leaving you every time you breathe out. Let it leave you.
   Experience this for several minutes, and it leaves you
   feeling relaxed.

5. Feel calmness in your body. Still your mind. Breathe in
   slowly and steadily. Hold your breath for two seconds then
   breathe out. Feel the stillness, begin to feel grounded,

anchored to the earth. Feel, through the heaviness of
your relaxed state, your connection to the earth, to divine
nature.

6. Relaxed, with tension drained away, tell yourself:

I am with the divine.
I am a part of divine nature.
I am not alone, but a
    part of, upon and surrounded
    by the divine.

7. Repeat these words several times.

This exercise, like everything else in life, will become progres-
sively clearer with practice.

CHAPTER 2

To Walk with Lions

Lion, for so long my thoughts have been clasped
by your paws and today your form stalks
through my mind.
Our spirits are merged in an indefinable way.

GARETH PATTERSON—*A Lion's Pride*

*B*orn a Leo in Britain of a Leo mother, I grew up in West, East and southern Africa. From a young age, the wilds drew me. I remember, when I was about four years old, walking off into the bush surrounding our house in northern Nigeria in search of a rainbow's end. My closest companions were my dog, Christo, and my African playmates.

At the age of seven my parents divorced. During that time I endured a short and traumatic period in a British boarding school. Mercifully, after just one term of incarceration, I was brought back to Africa. My mother remarried and sometime afterwards we, my mother, my stepfather, and I, went on "safari." We traveled to East Africa, where I witnessed lions upon the Serengeti plains, lions aloft and lazing in trees at Lake Manyara. I will always remember the sight of a very old male lion in the Ngorongoro Crater. His body was thin, his face crumpled, and yet, there in the shade of an umbrella tree, he held enormous dignity.

These, though, were not the first lions that I had seen in my young life. I had seen lions twice before. Those two very contrasting occasions had moved me, and had instilled within me an early understanding of right and wrong with regard to man and wild animals.

The first time I saw wild lions I was in the Yankari Game Reserve in Nigeria. One morning, as we bumped through the bush in a game drive truck with other visitors, I suddenly saw two lions, a male and a female. The lions appeared to be a part of the land around them, gorgeously tawny in the sun-drenched surroundings. Only their leonine outlines defined them as entities upon the land and not the very land itself. Without their outlines they would have been a brush stroke of gold upon a great natural canvas.

I called to the adults, "Look, lions!" At first they thought I was merely playing a child's game. Then someone else saw the lions and the vehicle came to an abrupt and undignified stop. Adults grabbed their cameras and binoculars and spoke very excitedly. "My" lions then rose and ran.

They left behind only their scuffed tracks, like a line of broken flowers upon the dust. The adults' emotion was excitement and disappointment rolled into one. The child, though, felt no loss, for he had been given a wonderful indelible memory—a memory of lions wild and free. I think that day a portion of my soul ran with the lions and has stayed with them ever since.

I next saw a lion several months later. One day, on "home leave" in Britain, my father collected me from my mother and stepfather to take me on an outing. He took me to the local zoo. The weather was gray and it was drizzling. I cannot remember what other animals I saw there, only the lion. I will always remember approaching a cage with thick metal bars, behind which was a concrete floor. The wall at the back of the cage was painted with a bright, ugly jungle scene. The artist had clearly not known that lions do not inhabit jungles.

Despite this flurry of color the atmosphere of the cage was depressing, almost morbid. Standing on the far side of the cage was a male lion. He was drenched by the rain, his mane ragged and matted. He looked nowhere with eyes that saw nothing. His eyes contained no fire of life and were simply devoid of emotion. His soul had died long ago and he stood with no purpose, for there was no purpose.

I remember almost recoiling at the sight of this lonely lion. To me it was an ugly sight. I felt that something I was looking at was wrong—in fact everything. Suddenly the image of "my" two lions flashed through my mind in glorious gold, then they were gone. I pulled at my father's arm for us to walk on. There, in that British zoo, I felt that I had seen the living dead—and on reflection today, I realize that that was indeed what I had seen.

That sight of the male lion in the zoo has never left me and never will. Seeing lions wild and free and then seeing the incarcerated lion instilled within me the beauty and the vitality of freedom—and the ugliness, the starving of the soul that is imprisonment. Today, reflecting on those two occasions always reinforces for me how essential it is that we must hold freedom in our hearts, for without it we slowly become like the bedraggled zoo lion. By seeking freedom in our hearts we can break free from the chains that shackle us to depression, the sense of purpose-lessness and loneliness of spirit. By finding that freedom we can bound powerfully and be untouchable like the Yankari lions.

Two or three years after I saw the zoo lion, my mother gave me a "game reserve." For two weeks before Christmas she and my stepfather had constructed a papier-mâché game reserve on a wide wooden board, in the evenings after I had gone to sleep. There, upon painted hills, plains and waterholes, stood an array of plastic animal species. The lion pride, complete with little cubs, was my favorite. That same Christmas my mother gave me a book. It was entitled *Bwana Game* by George Adamson.[16] George was the husband of Joy Adamson, who had enthralled readers worldwide with the story of the lioness Elsa in her book *Born Free*.[17] I was gripped by George's stories, by his adventures in northern Kenya as a game warden. I would constantly, with close scrutiny, examine the pictures in the book of George and his manmade pride of orphan lions.

When I look back into the past, I can see that certain proc-
esses had taken place. I believe that as a child I had unconsciously
affirmed to myself what I was to do in the future. I allowed myself to identify so much with George's book and many others
about African wildlife (particularly the lion) that, in a sense, I
was steering myself toward my own eventual life with and for
lions. From a young age I devoured such books, rereading them
countless times, and each time was an affirmation to myself of
what I would do one day. Also, I believe it is no coincidence that
in turn I am today a writer of books about the African wilds. I
began writing, my first book at the age of twenty-one. When I was
twenty-five it was published, and six more books followed in
twelve years.

Books and lions. As a child I had projected my future, and
after George Adamson's death in 1989 a series of events placed
me in a position to continue his work. I rescued his last lion
orphans and lived as a human member of this small pride, steering them into the wilds and freedom.

As I entered my early teens, we moved to the lovely country
of Malawi. There I increasingly became a young rebel "lion." I
rebelled against conventional expatriate life, that of only mix-
ing with other "expats," of the golf-club scene and the constant
talk about "home" (Britain). I *was* home, Africa was home; and
though my friends were of many hues and nationalities, the majority were Africans. While my mother, stepfather and brother
played golf with their fellow expat friends, I was usually among
the mountains and hills with my friend Charles and my dog Coco.
Charles lived in a large village close to where we lived and together we would explore along rivers and streams, even pan-
ning for what we thought was gold. I had freedom.

We knew intimately a portion of a mountain range called
Michiru. We knew where the shy duikers (a small antelope
species) lived and upon which slopes the klipspringers could be

found—and the baboons, well, I think they got to know us better than we knew them, and they would bark down at us from the rocky crevices.

Charles, Coco and I spent entire days in those hills and mountains. In the evening, exhausted, we returned to a hill close to where I lived. At dusk, we sat and watched the sun set over the Michiru Mountains. The day ended as the last light filtered away and night began. "Bye, Charles," I would say. "Bye, Garathee," he would reply. Charles would then disappear down the hill to the village below and Coco and I would slowly make our way to the house.

During my early teens, perhaps as a way to tame the young rebel lion within me, I was sent to a boarding school in southeast England to finish my schooling. Away from Africa, Coco, Charles and my other friends, I initially felt incarcerated, subjugated and alone. New to their ways and culture, I was the brunt of some of the schoolboys' jokes and insults. I did not cope well and missed Africa achingly. My unhappiness manifested in my developing an eating disorder. I ate more than would be considered normal, and usually it was stodgy foods and sweets. Not uncommonly I would force myself to vomit after a meal. The first term of school seemed to go on forever, but finally it ended and I returned to Malawi, the sun, Coco, Charles and the mountains.

One afternoon during the holidays I discussed my feelings of alienation in Britain with two good Malawian friends of mine. Both were at least ten years older than I was and I think they regarded me as a younger brother. A few days later, my two friends came to the house and announced that they had some traditional medicine. They told me that I needed protection and that they had consulted a traditional healer. They then asked me if I would use the medicine and I said yes. A little later, upon the hill near the house, a small ceremony took place. A brand-new razor blade was taken from its paper packaging and tiny incisions were made on both my shoulders. The dark-colored medicine (a combination of various herbs, I was told) was then inserted into the incisions. The medicine, once positioned, became a part of me. The tiny incisions seemingly just closed, holding the medicine within, without any scabs subsequently appearing. The incisions just closed.

When I returned to England I felt strengthened. I felt that I was carrying a part of Africa within me through the protective medicine. I became increasingly drawn to anything relating to Africa: books and television programs, African music and related music such as reggae. I also learned of the Rastafarian religion and of the Lion of Judah. And I wrote frequently to my Malawian friends.

My confidence grew increasingly, and as it did I left stodgy food and sweets behind. I started to eat salads and uncooked foods as much as possible. The induced vomiting stopped. I worked out daily, took up long-distance running and did light weight training with friends in the evening. I also began to read up on herbalism and I studied numerology. I was transforming myself by believing in myself.

Toward the end of my school days, with just a term to complete, I began to consciously "plan" my future in Africa. Unconsciously, though, as I understand it today, I was affirming at the time things that were still very far off. One late afternoon, as I sat in a cold classroom with the rain lashing down at the windows, I wrote a letter. It was a letter to an old man who lived with lions and whose adventures had first inspired me half of my young life ago. I wrote to George Adamson, telling him of my love of and passion for the wilds and how I wished to learn from him and to be his assistant.

During the following holiday I received a letter from Kenya that had been forwarded from the school by a kindly housemaster. The letter was a reply not from George, but, to my great surprise, from his wife Joy. She wrote:

Your letter to my husband was sent to my address. As
I know that he doesn't need an assistant, I am offering
you to assist me in my leopard research. To assist me
you will have to help me locating the very strongly
imprinted female leopard that roams utterly free
across 150 square kilometers ... but trusts me and is
very affectionate to me.

Joy also wrote in the letter about the conditions where she
was undertaking the rehabilitation of the leopard, called Penny.
She wrote of how she lived "in tents inside a fenced-in compound.
Often lions, buffalo and elephants are close [by]. Shaba [National
Reserve] is hot, near the equator and 3000 feet [in] altitude."

To me it sounded fantastic and I could not believe that she
would have even considered me as a possible candidate for her
assistant in the leopard project. I wrote back enthusiastically. I
explained that I had a term of school to complete but would
indeed like to undertake the position of her assistant.

Today, I do not know whether or not Joy ever received my
reply. Tragedy was about to unfold in the Kenyan bush. Joy Adamson was murdered a month after she sent her letter to me. News
of her death arrived almost immediately after I had returned to
England to complete my final term. On arriving at Heathrow
Airport I bought a newspaper, and the headline leapt up at me.
It read "Joy Adamson dead." Joy had been murdered on the evening of January 3, 1980. A disgruntled ex-employee had stabbed
her to death.

The world had lost an exceptionally talented and tenacious
woman, a woman who brought to the world the story of *Born
Free*, a story that evoked new consciousness and awareness about
African wildlife in general and about one species in particular,
the lion.

Two weeks later I received a sad, simple and straightforward
letter from a representative of Joy's company, Elsa Ltd. It read:

Dear Mr. Patterson,

    In view of the circumstances, you will appreciate that there is no need to follow up on Mrs. Adamson's letters.

My career in wildlife began in South Africa, at a private game reserve bordering the world-famous Kruger National Park. South Africa was not the Africa I knew. It was in those days a place of First World infrastructure and an outrageous, prejudiced white mentality. The apartheid government enchained the majority of the nation and kept people apart on the basis of color.

I started my career at the bottom—well, as near to the bottom as a white could start in that old South Africa, which is just above the blacks. My duties included carrying the game lodge's guests' luggage to their rooms, cleaning the swimming pool and transporting refuse from the lodge to the dump.

Later I took on a post in the Drakensberg Mountains where, together with a friend, I established an environmental education wilderness trails center. After a year or so, I headed north and entered the lion realm of the Tuli bushlands in Botswana. There at Tuli I was encouraged to undertake a study of the Tuli lion population, of which little was known at the time.

As a ranger-guide in Tuli I became totally engrossed in the lions' world, studying the prides of the region. The king of the Tuli bushlands was Darky, a magnificent black-maned lion. Darky was accepting of my presence in a land where lions were at best watchful and, at worst, fearful of man. Darky's acceptance of me was a window from which I could intimately view and understand the lions of Tuli. I regard him as my lion father, an almost mystical lion who taught me so much about his kind. There in Tuli I also learned much about the threats to the African lion.

I witnessed firsthand the effects of poaching and illegal hunting on the lion population. Almost 50 percent of the Tuli lion population died at the hand of man in a short two-and-a-half-year period. The major reason why the lions died was simply because man was not affording them adequate protection—a chronic dilemma that exists not uncommonly in many places in Africa.

Finally, after three years, I left the area to rewrite, in desperation, the book I was working on in the hope that upon its publication it would create awareness and, in turn, concern and greater preservation for the Tuli lions.

After completing the book, with my eyes now wide open to the dangers facing the African lion, I set off on a twenty-five-thousand-kilometer journey of discovery through southern Africa to learn of the history, present status and potential future of the lions of that region. This project culminated in my writing a second book[18] and in my meeting George Adamson for the first time.

During my travels into the last of the lions' range in southern Africa, I wrote to George telling him of my lion study in Tuli and of the current project. I received a reply from his remote camp, Kampi ya Simba in the Kora National Reserve, and an invitation to visit him. Soon after I received the reply, my first book, *Cry for the Lions*,[19] was published and I sent George a copy of it.

At the end of my travels in southern Africa I flew to Kenya and then, guided by a tattered hand-drawn map that I had obtained, drove to the Kora National Reserve. It was a revelation meeting George. For the very first time I was meeting a man who shared my concern for the continental plight of the African lion.[20] George was a rare pioneer at that time in the realization that the African lion was already endangered and under threat.

My visit to George was short. But at its end the old man invited me to return to Kora when I had completed writing my new book, and to work with him. This I did. I returned within three months and stayed there for half a year. I often monitored George's wild pride, a pride consisting of second- and third-generation descendants of lions that George had rehabilitated in the past. I also found a lion that had been long presumed dead. At the time, George had adopted three very small orphaned cubs named Batian (the male) and Rafiki and Furaha (the two sisters).

At the age of eighty-two, George was devoted to ensuring that the three cubs would one day find their freedom back in the wild. He loved the cubs deeply and I feel that they triggered within him memories of Elsa's story and the story of the many other lions that he successfully returned to the wilds over many years.

Toward the end of my time at Kora, George expressed the wish that he wanted me to work full-time with him and "after me," "to make sure that Kora does not collapse." This was an enormous honor. Deep within me, however, intuition told me that I was not destined at that time to continue working at Kora. Sometimes I could almost hear Tuli calling me. Strange as it might seem, I chose to leave Kora but did so with sadness in my heart.

A strange incident took place when I left and drove for the final time from Kora back to Nairobi. Two hours into the journey, I suddenly felt a pain and a simultaneous crash on my chest. I immediately looked down and there lay a lifeless dove. Somehow the dove had flown through the open window on my right and died upon impact with my chest. I thought then that it was a sign, but at the time could not think of what. Today, I believe that it was a sign of an enormous tragedy that was to take place in the months ahead.

After leaving Kenya I divided my time between writing a book about my experiences at Kora[21] and planning a new lion project in Tuli. The book was written in tribute to George and his work. As I wrote, I looked forward to sending George, upon completion, a copy of the manuscript for his comment and approval. The main objectives of "the Tuli Lion Project" I was planning were to continue further lion research, and to ensure the greater protection of the Tuli lions and all wildlife in that region. I also planned to run low-volume wilderness trails to assist in financing the first two objectives.

As I reached the completion of the book, and received permission to establish a camp in the northwestern part of the Tuli, a producer from an Australian documentary company contacted me. They proposed making a program on George and me, and it was planned that I would return to Kora for filming around about the third week of August.

One evening at the end of July, as I sat among friends discussing aspects of the proposed Tuli Lion Project, I suddenly said, "I have a strange feeling that I am going to walk with lions in Tuli." My conscious self was interpreting my intuition that, with the new lion project, Tuli lions might accept me to the extent that I would be able to observe them on foot, rather than by Land Rover. Instead, my statement was a premonition.

On August 20, 1989 George Adamson was gunned down and killed by shifta bandits (poachers). The killing bullet came from behind, leaving a massive wound in George's chest. Remember the dove that died on my chest those months earlier?

When the phone rang and I first heard the news of George's death I dropped the handset. I was numb with utter disbelief, then shock set in. Days later, through the mist of shock, I heard myself asking no one but myself, "What about Kora now?" The question was answered in a newspaper report. Due to the volatile security situation Kora was to be closed indefinitely. People asked me, "What about George's cubs, what is their future now?"

I pulled myself together by focusing on the issue of the cubs. I learned through a series of telephone calls to Kenya that their future was uncertain. It seemed that the only solution for them was captivity, the total antithesis of what George had wished for his last three orphans. Upon hearing this, an idea began to hatch in my mind. After going through the logistics of my plan, I approached the Kenyan and Botswanan authorities and potential sponsors with the proposal for me to go to Kora and relocate George's cubs to the Tuli bushlands. At Tuli, I would continue George's work in rehabilitating the lions back into the wilds.

Incredibly, this plan (not without many worries and problems) was transformed into reality. I successfully moved the lions and settled into the Tuli with them. For almost four years I lived with the lions. It was an almost surreal life. I hunted, played, rested and defended territory with my small pride. On one occasion the lions saved my life from the attack of an enraged leopard, and upon the birth of cubs both lionesses led me to their newborns, I was part of the pride and I saw life through lions' eyes This experience, living as a human member of a lion pride, allowed me the privilege of entering a dimension of lion life that one would not have thought possible. The essence of the relationship between my lions and me was based on mutual empathy, trust and love.

It was also destined that I would be challenged by enormous tragedies, tragedies that could have totally broken me, and almost did. Batian, my beloved lion son, was lured out of the reserve and shot dead by trophy hunters. Furaha and two cubs were shot dead for a crime they did not commit. They were accused of killing a man. Within only hours they were charged, tried and then sentenced to death. This left only Rafiki, and her future, too, was threatened by man. Certain people in the area wanted her removed from the bushlands. I sensed, though, that it was in fact my "watchdog" presence that was to be removed from the area.

In order to protect her (and the cubs that she had just given birth to) I made the decision to leave the area, and I have not seen my last lion daughter since. But it was the right decision. Rafiki lived on, her cubs had cubs and today, as I write this, she is twelve years old and a grandmother.

I wrote two books about those profound times, *Last of the Free* and *With My Soul Amongst Lions*.[22] It has been my enormous privilege that these two books have been published in some twenty-one editions and fourteen different languages. My lions' story has inspired countless people from all over the globe and I have received literally hundreds of letters from readers who were touched by the lions' story. I believe that my lions were destined to inspire. This was their role and, despite the tragedies, enormous good and great awareness have been achieved. I learned so much from those times, and continue to do so. Those lessons are, after all, the essence of this book.

After I left the Tuli, I wrote my second book on my life with the lions. After this, I continued my fight for the African lion. I investigated the South African trophy hunting industry and researched specifically into a sordid practice known as "canned lion hunting," the shooting of captive-bred lions for sport. During my research I gained damning video evidence of a lioness being shot for sport near her young cubs, and this footage in turn contributed to an international exposé of such hunting.[23]

Just after I completed a book on this subject, which was to further expose the South African canned-lion hunting industry,[24] I was informed that thirty baby Tuli elephants had been kidnaped from their families by game capturers and sold to an animal broker in South Africa. I was involved in exposing this scandal too. Later, hard video evidence was obtained showing that the so-called "training" of the young elephants included cruel beatings. When this was exposed, the local and international response from the public was even greater than that after the canned-lion exposé. Since then fourteen of the young elephants have been liberated and live free among elephant family herds in a South African national park.

I have been involved in many other wildlife issues and projects. One such project was co-founding Lion Haven, southern Africa's first natural habitat sanctuary, for four orphaned lions that could not be returned to the wilds. Lion Haven is situated in a beautiful game reserve in the Western Cape Province in South Africa. The lions live in an one-hundred-ninety-eight-acre sanctuary upon a stunning plateau. West of Lion Haven are the Cape Mountains and to the east lies the Indian Ocean. Here live four very happy and contented lions.

With lessons in life comes realization. By mid-1999 it was clear to me that it was time to move away from being at the heart of wildlife issues in southern Africa and time to concentrate on developing and writing this book. I realized the enormous historical, and at times religious, connection between man and lions. The lion is an animal we can all identify with and one, I hope, who will help you—as he has helped me—to have a growing empathy for the divine nature upon which we live, which surrounds us and of which we are a part.

CHAPTER 3

The Lion & Us

This Nature is none other than God in things ... Animals and plants are living effects of Nature; Whence all of God is in all things ... Think thus, of the Sun in the crocus, in the narcissus, in the heliotrope, in the cockerel, in the lion ... To the extent that one communicates with Nature, so one ascends to Divinity through Nature.

GIORDANO BRUNO (1548-1600), burnt alive
by the Inquisition for his beliefs[25]

The lion is an immensely powerful symbol, far more powerful I believe than is understood in this modern age. Today, despite not having the ancient knowledge of the lion's true power, we still draw on its symbolism, be it in art, advertising, corporate logos, branding or in the names of sports teams. We are subconsciously drawn to the lion—and this should not be surprising. The lion has had more impact on the traditions and beliefs of man than any other animal. The true depth of the relationship between man and the lion might be revealed one day, and should this occur, I feel we will discover the mysterious ancient religious significance of the lion.

From the Paleolithic age to ancient Egyptian times and from those times to this day, the lion and its symbolism have been a part of human history, and a significant relationship has existed between mankind and the lion. Profiles, for example, of lions were etched in cave walls in France more than fifteen thousand years ago. According to D. J. Conway, in her book *The Mysterious, Magickal Cat*,[26] these caves were symbolic "of the body of the Great Goddess," and "In a huge cave in Pech-Merle in France is a painting of a red human-lion figure, wearing a crown; called the Lion Queen [...] In the foothills of the Pyrenees stands a cave, Les Trois Frères, containing the Chapel of the Lioness; on a stone altar is carved a lioness and her cub. This lioness has been termed 'the Guardian of Initiation.'" A fairly recent discovery at Hollenstein (Germany) was an intriguing and mysterious ivory statuette with a lioness's head on a human body—and it is thought that this statuette could even predate the cave paintings.

The lion is the most frequently mentioned non-domestic animal in the Bible, and is referred to over one hundred and forty times. In a recent paper, one Christian writer stated: "Lions are important to God ... my suspicion is that God chose the likeness of a lion to convey to us a bit of his character. This is the real reason we have always seen power and authority in this animal."[27] Indeed, God likens himself to a lion in Hosea 5: 14, where he states: "For I will be unto Ephraim as a lion, and as a young lion to the house of Judah." In the Book of Amos (3: 3-8) God says:

> Can two walk together, except they be agreed? Will
> a lion roar in the forest, when he hath no prey?
> will a young lion cry out of his den, if he have taken
> nothing? ... Surely the Lord God will do nothing, but
> he revealeth his secret unto his servants the prophets.
> The lion hath roared, who will not fear? the Lord
> God hath spoken, who can but prophesy?

The very power of Jesus is likened to that of a lion in the Book of Revelation, 5: 5: "Weep not, behold, the Lion of the tribe of Juda." In Proverbs 30: 30, it is written of the King of Beasts, "A lion which is strongest among beasts, and turneth not away for any."

The lion in certain parts of Africa is also associated with God and is considered "to be God's manifestation in His immanent aspect," according to the scholar John S. Mbiti.[28]

The ancients of the Near East deified the lion. In what was Mesopotamia the lion was among the animal gods, and other gods were often depicted riding or standing upon lions. In ancient

Persia, stone lions were used to decorate the graves of the bravest Bakhtiari warriors. In the ancient Egyptian cities of Leontopolis (which literally means "City of the Lion") and Heliopolis (City of the Sun), lions were kept as sacred animals, living symbols of gods on earth. In the temple of Amun Ra at Heliopolis, lions were cared for by the highest-ranking priests. There were laws that decreed full public mourning on the death of one of the lions, and the lion's body would be embalmed and entombed with the greatest ceremony.

Ramses II, described as "the greatest King that ever ruled over Egypt," went into battle accompanied by a lion called Auto-m-nekht. The lion ran alongside the chariot and knocked down anyone who tried to attack the ruler. According to Charles Guggisberg's pioneering book about the lion, *Simba*, the ancient Egyptian hieroglyphic symbol for the seasonal flooding of the Nile valley was a lion's head, which is "probably owing the fact that the Nile began to rise when the sun was in the constellation of the lion. Could this possibly also be the reason why in much more recent times so many drinking fountains were ornamented with lions' heads?"[29]

The ancient Egyptians regarded Atum, the oldest creator god, the original sun god, as being leonine in one form. The creator god, in turn, created Shu, the air god, and Tefnut, the moisture goddess, who first took shape as a pair of lion cubs and grew into the two lions who guarded the eastern and western horizons. The goddesses Sekhmet (called by the ancient Egyptians "the mighty one" or "the one of great magic"), Hathor, Mehyt, Qekesh, Bast (or Bastet) and others had leonine forms or associations. Sekhmet, the lioness goddess, could rage yet at the same time was mistress of healing who drove away sickness.

Today, Sekhmet and Bast are probably the best-known leonine ancient Egyptian goddesses. Bast was the daughter of the sun god Ra and was known as the lady of the east because of her as-

sociation with the rising sun. Bast, originally portrayed as a lioness, was worshiped for over three thousand years (and is still
worshiped by many pagans and others even today). Bast was
one of the "eyes of Ra," an avenger goddess sent by Ra to destroy
the enemies of Egypt and her gods. The center of the Bast cult
was in Bubastis, located north of Giza on the eastern side of the
Nile. It was there that early archaeologists in the mid-nineteenth
century discovered the burial place of hundreds of thousands of
mummified holy cats.

Bast was the goddess of fire, the moon, fertility, childbirth,
pleasure, dance, protection from disease, of intuition, healing and
of all animals (especially cats).[30] She is stated to be the mother
of the lion god Mithos, who was depicted as a lion-headed man
carrying a large knife. Mithos was invoked to protect the inno-
cent and to punish transgressors of "maat" (truth).

Lion symbolism prevailed in ancient Egyptian times. The
lion was among the animal figures most commonly found in
Egyptian art. The lion was the guardian against unseen forces.
Entrances to the temples, palaces, tombs and the royal throne
were guarded and protected by images of the lion. The belief
that man needed to be protected at night while asleep led the
ancient Egyptians to decorate their beds with motifs of the lion.
Also the heads of the funeral biers were carved in the shape of
a lion's head, symbolizing the Aker lions, the double lion gods
of yesterday and tomorrow, which protected the afterlife. The
Aker sphinx-lions were closely identified with the enigmatic
Akeru, the "Lion People," said to have been the gods on earth
in predynastic Egypt.

It has been written that "The Egyptian priests in many cer-
emonies wore the skins of lions which were symbols of the
great solar orb" and that "initiates of the Egyptian Mysteries were
sometimes called lions. The lion was the emissary of the sun,
symbolizing light, truth and regeneration."[31]

Lying exactly on the 30th parallel north, at the center of the earth's landmasses, is the most enduring leonine symbol of all time, the Sphinx. The Sphinx, symbolic of strength and wisdom, was known to the ancient Egyptians as Hor-em-Akhet, meaning "Horus in the Horizon."[32] The lion was a sacred animal to the god Horus. The Sphinx was originally dated to 4000 BC, but interestingly some researchers today are suggesting that is far older, and that when first created in 10500 BC it directly faced the constellation of Leo, the Lion, just before sunrise.

Hundreds of kilometers south of the Sphinx, in what is today Sudan, existed the Kingdom of Kush,[33] the kingdom of the Lion God. Little known about even today, Kush has been described as "one of the most tantalizing mysteries of antiquity"— an urban, civilized and literate African state ... and the lion was sacred there too. Apedemek, "the lord of royal power," was a Kushitic lion god, and at the Lion Temple at Naga, south of Meroë, reliefs show Apedemek worshiped by the royal family. The kings were always seated upon lion thrones. Temple reliefs show the enemies of the king subdued by, and in some cases devoured by, lions. It has been stated that lions were kept in the lion temple, as living symbols of Apedemek. Interestingly, research has revealed that the worship of the ancient Egyptian lioness goddess, Sekhmet, could have been originally introduced into Egypt from Sudan. One wonders what other leonine-related mysteries exist unrevealed and unknown at the sites of the civilization of Kush.

The lion of ancient times was also a symbol of wisdom. King Solomon was at times symbolized as a lion. In the first Book of Kings (10: 19-20) Solomon's throne is described: "The throne had six steps, and the top of the throne was round behind: and there were stays [handrests] on either side on the place of the seat, and two lions stood beside the stays. And twelve lions stood there on the one side and on the other upon the six steps: there was not the like made in any kingdom."

Intriguingly, the modern-day Rastafarian religion, which has had a phenomenal growth since the mid-1970s, also has its roots in the land of the Nile valley. Ra, the Egyptian sun god, is viewed as the life-giving force. It has been written that "At the heart of Rastafari lies the Egyptian mysteries, the sort that may be found in the *Egyptian Book of the Dead* ... the elements of Judaism within Rastafari are themselves the offspring of Egyptian mysticism."

Lion symbolism is omnipresent in Rastafari. Viewed as the Messiah, the late Ethiopian Emperor Haile Selassie was "the Lion of Judah." Haile Selassie was born on July 23, the beginning of the astrological sign of the lion—Leo. The dreadlocks of the Rastafarians are also a part of the lion symbolism: they represent the mane of the lion (of Judah). Throughout his rule, Halle Selassie kept a collection of lions at his palace and two lions often flanked the emperor when he gave audiences.

The Basotho and Tswana of southern Africa have a name for the lion that is as intriguing as it is mysterious. They call the lion "tau," meaning "the star creature" or "the creature that came from the stars." In Botswana, where I lived with the Adamson lions, the country's president is traditionally known and honored as Tautona, meaning "the Greatest Lion." The traditional name that was given to me was Ra de Tau, "the Man of Lions" or "Father of Lions."

Murry Hope explains in her book *Ancient Egypt* that the Aker lion gods "later emerged in Theban times as the Twin Lion Gods ... Their names were Sef and Tuau."[34] Notice the similarity between the name Tuau and the Tswana word for lion, tau. The word tau also represents one of the most ancient forms of the cross, the Tau cross. The ancient Egyptian loop-topped version of the Tau cross, the "ankh," was known as "the cross of life," "the key to the mysteries" and "the key of life." Ros*tau* is the ancient name applied to the Necropolis at Giza, and is also the name of the center of the Duat, the ancient Egyptian underworld, which in turn was protected by the two Aker lion gods. Incidentally, the Tswana word "ra" has similar connotations to the Egyptian word "ra," which means "lord" or "master"—and in Egyptian art, a lion with a solar disc represented the god Ra.

According to the African shaman, wise man and historian Credo Mutwa, a Zulu term for the lion is "ibhubezi," coming from the verb "ibebeza," which means "making the final decision," supporting the universal belief that the lion is the king of the animals.[35] Mutwa has written that the Zulu people have a saying that "where a lion goes, there shall the bush be green,"[36] meaning "where a person of peace goes, there shall be great peace flowing around him." Credo has also recorded that, historically, African people believed that if the lion, leopard and other catlike animals disappeared from the face of the earth, "a great spiritual darkness would descend upon all life."

In the traditional African environmental-religious experience, every tribe had an animal species that was regarded as its totem, its sacred tribal emblem. Clans of the lion exist and existed in many parts of Africa. Gerhard Lindblom, the Swedish ethnographer, saw a wonderful example of the Kamba totem system concerning the lion in Kenya, in the early part of the twentieth century.[37] One late afternoon Lindblom shot an antelope, and after the meat was cooked and eating had begun a lion began roaring a few hundred meters away. Lindblom was surprised when one of the porters who were accompanying him suddenly took a large piece of meat and walked into the darkness in the direction of the lion.

When he returned, the Swedish scientist asked him what he had been doing. The porter replied, "You heard the lion roaring? I belong to the lion clan and I heard a kinsman calling me. He was hungry, old and feeble. Is it not my duty to share with him my meat when I sit here by the fire in comfort and have more meat than I can manage to eat?"

Early white travelers into what was then Bechuanaland (now Botswana) in southern Africa were astonished that the people literally protected lions who, in turn, provided them with meat. In a part of southern Africa that is now called KwaZulu/Natal, explorer William Charles Baldwin observed how the Tsonga people protected lions.

> Off at sunrise and saw three lions sneaking off from a wildebeest. I was anxious to go after the former, but the Amatonga would not hear of such folly and danger, and argued the matter thus, "What should I do with one (a lion) in case I was fortunate enough to kill?" ... *besides, the lions were their friends ... and they would have no part in molesting them.*[38]

Lions have historically been used for healing in Africa and beyond. D. J. Conway described in her book *The Mysterious, Magickal Cat* how in the Middle Ages the image of the lion was said to have great healing power. Doctors, Conway wrote, would prescribe that their patients carry or wear a piece of jasper (a red, yellow, dark green or brown variety of quartz) carved with the image of a lion to cure fevers and to protect against poison. Additionally, if a lion was carved on a garnet, it supposedly cured all diseases and protected the wearer, while the engraved lion's head was said to impart strength. In Africa, the lion's fat is said to have healing and protective properties.

Sir Alfred Pease, an author of one of the early modern books on the lion,[39] had a strange encounter with a sacred healing lion in Algeria in 1892. He was traveling in a carriage when he saw what he thought was a fully grown dead lion being transported on a donkey's back led by a party of Arabs. He stopped the carriage, jumped out and ran after this party, calling them to halt. He asked them where they had killed the lion. "*Mackash mot*," one Arab replied, "Not dead"—and to his astonishment the lion was instructed to climb off the donkey's back. The lion was old, blind but otherwise perfectly healthy. The Arabs informed him that this was a sacred lion that was taken from area to area, village to village, to exorcize evil spirits, to cure the sick and to drive away disease.

This story, from little more than a hundred years ago, is intriguing as it reminds one of the association of the goddess Cybele with the lion. Lions were kept in the temples of this mother goddess in ancient Greece. The high priests of Cybele wandered the country with their tame lions, which they used in exorcizing rituals. Incidentally, early Arabs had a deity called Yaghuth who was a lion god and it was considered that the lion was a protector against evil.

The lion is everywhere! In China, for example, where the lion was not even indigenous, it was one of the four sacred animals of power. Representing strength, courage and energy, the lion was said to watch over and protect the living and the dead. (The Pekinese dog was bred specially to resemble a lion and hence be a guardian figure.)

In India, the lion was the mount of the great goddess Durga, as she rode to destroy demons. The Royal Throne, Sinhasana, means "the seat of the Lion." It has been said the lion "has played a major part in the symbols and folklore of Indian culture for more then two thousand years."[40] The fourth incarnation of Vishnu, a major Hindu god, was Nrsimha (Narasimha, the "Tawny One" or "ManLion"). The Greek sun god Apollo was also identified with the lion, and the Greek god Eros was depicted riding a lion. The emblem of the Persian religion of Mithraism was a lion's head surrounded by a mane of sun rays. A grade level of their initiates was called a "lion" and "the son of God" Mithra was depicted ascending to heaven in the form of a lion, and was also often portrayed as a winged lion.

Of the founder of the Islamic sect of Bektash, Haji Bektash Wali, it was written "*he rode lions*, talked with birds and deer, *walked on the sea, flew to the heavens on a lion's skin*, raised the dead, gave sight to the blind and cured the sick." In South America the figure of the sun god Viracocha at Tiahuanaco, in modern Bolivia, has been described as having "the features of a lion, it faces due east."[41]

A god, goddess or person depicted between two lions is potent symbolism. The goddess Ishtar of Babylon was often depicted standing with two lions. In the ancient Babylonian "Hymn to Ishtar" it is written:

O lioness from heaven, bring me peace
And rest and comfort, hearken to my prayer!
Is anger pity, may thine eyes look down with
    tenderness and blessings, and behold
Thy servant.

A seal ring from Crete shows a great goddess figure standing between guardian lions. At the entrance to the Acropolis of Mycenae (Greece) is the famous Lion Gate, with two great lions carved in rock between the entrance. This intriguing use of lions in symbolism is thought to be the oldest of its kind in Europe (c. 1250 BC).

It has been written that "The sheer physical power of the lion kept its suggestion of divinity right through ancient Mesopotamia to Greek and Roman civilization and finally Christian art."[42] Look around you in Europe and America and see where the dual lion gods stand as two stone lion statues. It is interesting that this powerful pagan symbol entered into Christian art in the West. In London, for example, statues of the lion are almost too numerous to mention. The most famous animal statues there are Landseer's Trafalgar Square lions—twenty feet long and eleven feet high. Lions are guardians at the entrance of the King Edward VII building at the British Museum and there are the Imperial College lions, the Marylebone Road lions, the York Water Gate lions, the South Bank lions ... and so on. The oldest outdoor statue in London, which dates from 1600 BC, is that of the lioness goddess Sekhmet in New Bond Street.

In English heraldry the lion is predominant. In fact, it seems that at the very birth of heraldry the lion was the symbolically favored emblem animal of the English royal family. The arms of England, first used by Richard I (Richard Coeur de Lion or Richard the Lion Heart), depict three lions and this imagery has been used by all subsequent sovereigns to the present day.

Hero figures of pre-dynastic Egypt were repeatedly shown between two wild animals. One depiction, that on the famous ivory knife handle found at Gebet-el-Arack, is particularly intriguing. The handle has been described as being "decorated with the image of a man heroically subjugating two huge lions."[43] On inspection of this image, I was immediately struck by the body language of the lions and the man. To me, having lived with lions, what was depicted here was not subjugation but fellowship. The lions' stance is not one of subjugation or of being dominated. To me, from my personal experience of being greeted by, and in turn having greeted lions, the lions of the knife handle are greeting a human friend ...

Intriguingly, this image of a man between two lions is almost identical in imagery to that in a fragment of an ancient Egyptian wall painting (from Heirakonopolis) dating to 3200 BC. The artists of ancient Egypt and the Near East shared, it seemed, an interpretation with regard to this image. Also most interestingly, within Judaism to this day, the lion symbolism is depicted on the scrolls of the Torah (seemingly protecting them).

Startling in its beauty, this ancient and rare Sumerian love poem illustrates how the very word "lion" was used as a term of endearment thousands of years ago.

> Bridegroom, dear to my heart,
> Goodly is your beauty, honeysweet.
> Lion, dear to my heart,
> Goodly is your beauty, honeysweet ...
> Bridegroom, let me caress you,

My precious caress is more savory than honey.
In the bedchamber, honey-filled,
Let me enjoy your goodly beauty.
Lion, let me caress you,
My precious caress is more savory than honey.
Bridegroom, you have taken your pleasure of me.
Tell my mother, she will give you delicacies.
Tell my father, he will give you gifts.
Your spirit, I know where to cheer your spirit,
Bridegroom, sleep in our house until dawn.
Your heart, I know where to gladden your heart,
Lion, sleep in our house until dawn.[44]

Is it not strange that the ability of a human to transform temporarily into another animal is so often associated with the large predators in many parts of the world? In Nordic countries there were the "bear people," who changed into bears. Historically, in Central Europe, stories of "werewolves" and "wolf men" abounded. In Sumatra and Java, the jungle people implicitly believed in the existence of tiger men, who turned temporarily into tigers, either purposely by means of magic or quite unconsciously. The Aztecs and Mayas of Mexico taught about the power of their shamans in becoming half-human and half-jaguar. In Western Africa and the Congo basin the phenomenon of the "leopard man" was well known and may persist to this day. According to Owen Burnham, in his book *African Wisdom*, the Papal people of Guinea Bissau believe that "they can transform themselves into many animals, including pythons and leopards. In this case, the transformation is believed to be a literal one and is achieved through a deep knowledge and understanding of the animal spirit involved."[45]

And what of men becoming lions in modern times? This might sound outlandish or fanciful, but I believe, as do many Motswana people, that some of the Bushmen could have this ability. I could recount how in olden times this phenomenon was reported, but rather wish to tell of a modern story of when men seemingly drew from the lion, to become lions and to hunt as lions.[46]

In 1982 a man called Ed Flattery, who farmed in the Ghanzi area of Botswana, had two of his cattle killed by lions on two separate occasions. After the second killing, Flattery and two of his Bushmen employees set off to follow the cattle-killing lions' tracks. I must add that Flattery had been brought up in the company of Bushmen and spoke their language. They followed the lion tracks until they were beyond the farmlands and the tracks led on into the expanses of the Kalahari.

Eventually, as they continued onwards, they saw smoke rising in the distance, in the direction in which the lion tracks were leading. At this point, Flattery's two Bushmen employees refused to continue, saying that it was not the lions that they were following but the Makaukau, members of a Bushmen clan who are known for their ability to transform into lions. They told Flattery that these Makaukau had turned themselves into lions to hunt during the night. Disbelieving, Flattery persuaded the Bushmen to continue, while he kept an eye on the lion tracks. The tracks led them to two small grass huts. Outside one was a fire, the source of the smoke that they had seen from afar. In the center of the cleared area, next to the huts, was a large pile of ash and it was toward this that the lion tracks led. The tracks crossed the ash—and then simply disappeared!

To Flattery's utter incredulity, no further tracks could be found. It was then that his employees pointed to the occupants of the grass shelter—two men, two women and a few children. Both the men were injured, one on the head and the other on the chest. To the Bushmen employees, this was evidence to prove their point. They were convinced that the men's injuries had been caused by the horns of the cattle they had been hunting.

I too have experienced situations that beg for explanation. At times during 1989 and 1990 I was somehow moving through the bush with my lions during the night, while at the same time I was fast asleep in my tent! Certain game rangers in the Tuli bushlands reported finding my tracks and those of the lions at sunrise on some mornings. These rangers are expert trackers, and from the signs that they found they were convinced that I had walked with the lions three or four hours previously—at night, in darkness.

Initially I greeted these reports with amusement, as there was no explanation of how I could move through the bush with three lions, far from my camp, in darkness. In addition, if this was elaborate sleepwalking, why was it that Julie, my girlfriend at the time, did nor hear me either getting up or returning what would have been quite some time later? During our three-and-a-half years together in the bush, Julie always woke up when I began to sleepwalk. We continued to receive reports of my nocturnal wanderings from time to time. Inwardly I was unsure of the truth of the reports, while outwardly I dismissed the stories. That was until the day I saw the tracks myself!

I knew the area intimately and certainly would have remembered where I had walked the previous day, but to my surprise, early one morning, I found my tracks and those of the lions deep in the bush, in an area where I had not walked with them for a very long time, and on inspecting the tracks, I saw that they were very fresh, appearing to have been imprinted just a few hours earlier!

When I returned to camp I told Julie of my astonishing findings, and neither of us could think of a plausible explanation. Over the following weeks, the situation occurred several times. I would be taken aback to find the tracks far from camp and certainly not where I had recently walked with the lions. Each time the tracks were very fresh and very definitely my boots' imprints. Strangely, what coincided with each discovery of new tracks was that on waking up on those mornings I would always feel tired.

There was another experience that I had involving lions for which a "normal" explanation cannot be found. It took place during a short visit to Britain during the period that I was working with George at Kora.

My mother and I went to a wildlife park to see the rare descendants of the Barbary lion, which has been extinct in the wild for almost a century. The wildlife park was fairly busy with visitors, and as we approached the lions' enclosure I decided to hold back until a large group of people moved away, because I wished to try and connect mentally with the lions without the distractions of other people being near to me. My mother and I watched at a distance as the group viewed a beautiful lioness who had a litter of small cubs. The lioness, born in captivity, completely ignored the people watching her.

As the group eventually moved away, we went forward. Suddenly, though, as we drew close, the lioness saw me and immediately became enraged, charging me and stopping just short of the enclosure fence. I was astonished by her reaction and moved away, leaving my mother where she was standing. The lioness continued to snarl for as long as she could see me. I moved behind a tree and other people moved to where my mother stood. Peeping from behind the tree, I saw that the lioness was once again oblivious to the people and seemed completely calm. When the people moved on, I rejoined my mother and, astonishingly, the lioness again leapt forward, snarling and charging at the fence. My mother was equally surprised and said, "What are you doing to her?" I led her away and replied, "I haven't even begun to speak to her yet, I have no idea why she's reacting to me like that!"

Whenever I tell this story, people suggest that as I had come to Britain directly from Kora and George's lions I had the scent of lions on me—hence the lioness's reaction. Believe me, I had had more than one thorough bath since I left Kora!

The answer to the lioness's repeated reaction to me lies, I believe, not in a logical explanation but rather on a metaphysical level. After spending so much intense time among lions at Kora, the lion aspect of my nature would have been very strong and apparent to her. She was, I believe, responding not to my physical self but to that aspect of my spiritual self. Her dramatic reaction was clearly that of a lioness attempting to defend her cubs from a threatening, foreign, non-pride male lion. This is the only explanation that I can give for this strange incident.

Last, the sound of jackal calls often prompts lions to call; it has been noticed that when jackals call at night I sometimes respond in my sleep and call as a lion does.

There is a wonderful modern example of the lion-hearted using a reference to the lion on a triumphant occasion. Upon Nelson Mandela's victorious release from imprisonment in 1989, he paid testament to the youth of South Africa who had contributed so much toward the struggle for freedom. Mandela earnestly praised "the young lions of the nation" and received huge applause from the masses while shouts of "Viva!" filled the air.

In terms of man's understanding of his very self, certain scientists suggest that more could be learned about the origins of man as a social animal by studying the social structures of lion prides and wolf packs than by studying primates.

The lion has an undeniably powerful personality. Its dramatic call reverberates through the dark wilds like a voice that carries from this plane to that of the spirit world. As Laurens van der Post wrote of the lion's call, "It is to silence what the shooting star is to the dark of the night."

Today, at a time of violence, and with horrific wars in central Africa and part of Europe, a time "when man's brutal nature is shocking, the predators, whom man of recent times accused of great savagery, are slowly emerging again in our understanding as benign creatures"[47]—through whom man could learn of his very self. It is there that answers as to where we went wrong might lie, as we shock ourselves with our own true brutality and inhumanity in this modern day.

I close this section of *To Walk with Lions* with these haunting words by Evelyn Ames, which fittingly describe the power of the lion and the inspiration man can draw from these magnificent beings:

> Lions are not animals alone; they are symbols and totems and legends, they have impressed themselves so deeply on the human mind, if not its blood, it is as though the psyche were emblazoned with their crest.[48]

CHAPTER 4

Tribal & Natural Wisdom in the Modern World

We must take a great spiritual step ... We must adopt the view of creation that was held not only by ancient Africans, but also by Native Americans and many other people of the ancient world; that creation is one great wonderful whole, one revolving sphere of the purest, greenest crystal, a sphere to be viewed from all sides as one thing, instead of a number of shattered fragments upon the dark desert of human folly.

CREDO MUTWA[49]

*I*n Africa every tribe was named after its totem animal. It was the sacred duty of everyone in the tribe to ensure that the animal after which they were named was protected and never harmed. It was also the sacred duty of the tribe never to harm any animal with which their totem animal coexisted. For example, if you were of the Zebra people, you would never harm the wildebeest, whose herds often live in association with the zebra.

African people would therefore strongly identify spiritually with their totem animal. A person, his name and his totem were in reality one of spirit. Among the Mbuti pygmies, it is believed that when one dies, one turns into one's totem animal. In fact it has been stated that some forty-seven African tribes are thought to believe in rebirth, after death, as animals.[50]

Here lie lessons for the modern man. Totem systems and similar beliefs overcome the species barrier, a barrier that is another form of Western separatist ideology. By identifying closely with another species, the species barrier disappears. We can reach out and touch our other, we can become the other, and the other us.

I crossed the species barrier with my lions and they with me. The lions, despite my being human and different in shape from them, accepted me totally as a member of the pride. In fact, knowing them as I do, I can also state that they accepted me without question, unconditionally.

I had a place and a purpose for them. Why else, when fully adult and independent of me for food, would they routinely seek me to greet me, then go again? Why would they gravitate to my camp on two occasions when I was quite ill—then leave when I was well again? Why would the lionesses have an enormous urge and need each time they gave birth to lead me to their litters of newborn cubs? Why did one lioness risk great injury to herself by defending me from an enraged leopard that was attacking me? The answer is because at a certain level I was them, they were me, we were one. We felt that the other belonged.

I empathized so greatly with them that I became them, and they recognized this, in turn, recognizing themselves in me. The fact that I did not look like them physically was of no consequence; the important factor was how I felt to them.

The totem belief system develops in the big picture an affinity between a person and his environment, regardless of what the sacred animal might be. By recognizing your totem you identify with the animal's inner nature and the external nature that surrounds it. A soul link is forged to both.

Lion People

Many readers will identify the lion as their sacred animal. This, after all, could be a major reason why they were drawn to this book. For those who intuitively feel an association or an affinity to the lion, finish reading this book, then expand your knowledge about this King of Beasts by turning to the list of suggested reading at the back. When you have read and learned more about the lion, and you feel the time is right, return to this section to try the following exercise.

Whether your sacred animal is the lion or another animal, once you have learned about its ways, strengths and unique qualities, you can imbue yourself with those aspects of the animal's power through meditation. For example, as we saw in Chapter 3, the lion has been associated throughout the ages with the qualities of strength, protection, healing, wisdom and—from my own personal experience—serenity. If the lion is your sacred animal, you can imbue yourself with these aspects of the lion's vitality and character through meditation.

To receive these aspects of power from your sacred animal (two are explained in detail below), attempt the following exercise.

1. Go to a quiet place, sit comfortably, close your eyes and begin to relax.

2. Breathe in deeply, hold your breath for two seconds, then breathe out.

3. Try to breathe like this throughout the meditation.

4. Visualize either a feather falling from high in the sky in slow circular motions to the ground: it falls ever so gracefully earthwards; or the view from under peaceful waters, a stone failing slowly through the water toward the seabed.

When you are totally at peace and relaxed, visualize your body being filled with the power you need from your feet upwards to the top of your head.

STRENGTH

1. Feel your body being filled with a lion or lioness's strength. Feel the strength flowing upward, to your waist, then up to your chest.

2. Strength flows into both your arms and up into your head. You radiate with the lion's strength and power. Maintain this visualization for several minutes.

3. Radiating with this power, thank your sacred animal, the lion, and feel gratitude toward him or her.

4. Open your eyes and luxuriantly stretch your body as cats and lions do.

HEALING

1. When you need to receive healing from the lion, after the feather falling/stone falling visualization (when you are at peace), visualize healing gold or white light entering your body through your feet. The light flows up into your body and fills you.

2. Filled with the healing light, visualize the portion of your body where you need the healing in particular.

3. Visualize that part of your body radiating with the healing light. Infuse that part of your body with light.

4. After several minutes of visualizing it, thank your sacred animal, the lion, honor him or her and feel gratitude for the healing.

5. Open your eyes and gently stretch your body.

When you wish to direct the healing power of the lion to someone else, visualize that person being covered from their feet upwards in the golden or white light of healing.

1. Visualize them finally radiating with the light.

2. After as many minutes as you can easily maintain the visualization, thank the lion for sending the healing.

3. Open your eyes and stretch your body slowly.

With practice, as you repeat the exercise, you will increasingly identify with the lion and in turn be energized by aspects of the lion's vitality. Remember that the main aspects you can absorb from the vitality of the lion are:

- Strength
- Protection
- Healing
- Wisdom
- Serenity

In broad terms, South Africa's President Thabo Mbeki identified himself as an African because of what he feels he is part of, in his now famous "African Renaissance" speech. He said: "I owe my being to the hills and the valleys, the mountains and the glades, the rivers, the deserts, the trees, the flowers, the seas and the ever changing seasons. I know that none dare challenge me when I say, I am an African."

By identifying ourselves with all that is natural, humility blossoms within us. Imagine what the collective effect would be if we could all identify ourselves with the natural. We would arrive at the state called coexistence; and I believe that people are increasingly yearning toward that state.

There is the Golden Rule of some, who tell themselves: "Do unto others as you would like to be done unto." I believe that the time has come to enlarge this commendable code. We should expand it to: "Do unto everything that lives as you would like to be done unto."

If we lived by that New Golden Rule, we would not only heal ourselves, but also begin to heal all that is around us. We are all one. The air I breathe is the same air a lion breathes and the same air that you breathe.

Returning to traditional African religious beliefs, there are many African religions, but what all the religions seem to share is "an awareness of the spiritual, invisible dimension of all life. Trees, rivers, streams, rain are more than merely things to be utilized. They have a spiritual quality which unites them to human beings in a greater cosmic whole."[51]

Africans were viewed in our recent past as being backward for seeing and acknowledging the spiritual dimension in both the animate and the inanimate. Now we in the West are reaching the point where we are realizing that the sacralization of nature, like that in Africa, is a reality.

Such holistic wisdom extends into all of African life, including healing. Unlike in the West, where for so long the spiritual and the physical have been separated (treating the symptoms and not the cause), in African belief the whole person, the body and mind, is acknowledged to be afflicted—and treatment begins by attending to the mind, followed by healing of the body. By treating the emotional cause comes healing.

Healing comes from within. If we attend to the emotional affliction, we can heal the physical. Lions (and wild animals in general) have the most incredible recuperative powers and man, I believe, can draw inspirational powers from the lion. In a lion research area in the Serengeti, in Tanzania, the following examples of the lions' self-healing, recuperative powers were observed. One male had sustained a wound in his forefoot. The wound became infected and the leg swelled until he could only limp slowly; but, in a period of thirteen days, he had made a full recovery. A nomadic male was severely bitten in the leg and clawed in the scrotum, and four days later he was almost unable to move. The lion then withdrew into some hills to heal and remained there without eating for twenty days; when he reappeared on the plains, his leg had healed. Another male was bitten through the nasal bones; he was fully recovered six weeks later. In other wild animals the inner healing power is equally remarkable. I know of a female leopard who sustained an injury that resulted in the loss of a hind leg. She recovered and went on to have several litters of cubs. I once knew of a three-legged hyena that recovered from his injury (probably caused by a poacher's snare) and hunted successfully with his clan.

I also know of an elephant that, horrendously, had almost his entire trunk severed by a poacher's trap. His short tusks were longer than what remained of his trunk. Fellow rangers and I thought that it might be kinder to put the elephant out of any further suffering. Incredibly, the terrible injury healed and the elephant adapted to his disability. Equally incredible, herd members put food into his mouth to help sustain him while he began to heal.

There are further examples of wild animals' recuperative powers and adaptability to injury. I have seen film footage of a hyena that survived successfully in the wild with only two front legs! I have also seen film footage of a vervet monkey that was surviving well in the wilds despite having totally no use of its hind legs.

I witnessed astonishing healing in my male lion, Batian, who sustained terrible injuries, including the total severing of his tail in a confrontation with two other males. This story of great courage and self-healing is told in Chapter 6.

With wild animals, the healing comes from within, not from drugs and medicines, upon which humans seem to have become dependent. Modern man has separated himself from the healing that can be drawn from within and has become mentally dependent upon receiving healing from external means, i.e. drugs. It often seems that, unlike the wild animals, we have lost the knowledge that we, each and every one of us, have the capacity to heal ourselves.

I lived among my lions in the wilds for four years, and I can hardly think of a single day that the lions exhibited signs of illness, apart from wounds that always healed quickly. This is not to say, of course, that wild animals don't get ill; but compared to us they have incredible recuperative powers, and we can learn from this.

Have you ever noticed that friends and colleagues often get sick when they have trouble in their lives? This is because of the disease in their lives. We so often dwell on "problems" that should not even be allowed to become problems, and in turn we fall ill. In my experience, lions, by contrast, live for the moment, live in the today; their lives have a vitality, a vital life force—and we should tap into our own vital life force and learn from the lion.

We can all not only heal ourselves, but also help heal others if we truly wish to (but only if the person who is ill wants to heal). I have personal experience of this. For several years I half acknowledged within myself that I might have the capacity to help heal people. Then one day, about three years ago, I had the chance to put this to the test. Out of the blue, a psychic medium friend of mine called me in distress. A close friend of hers had fallen into a coma after a long illness; because of her closeness to him she felt that she could not successfully direct healing to him. Healing, it seemed, was blocked by her emotional state, and she asked me to attempt to send him healing.

I had had very little experience with this, and I knew little about the man except that he was a Native American, but I told her I would try. So I went outside and walked for about ten minutes to a peaceful spot on a hillside. I sat on a small termite mound and began to meditate. I calmed myself, closed my eyes and breathed in and out, long and deeply. When I had attained that heavy warm feeling in my solar plexus, I "saw" in my mind what I refer to as "lights of healing," two rays of light, which joined at a central point. I later "saw" a black-and-white photograph of a dark-haired man wearing a military-type uniform. Toward the end of my meditation I also saw a soaring bird, then the form of a man and an "aura" of white healing cloaking his body.

Afterward, feeling a little fatigued, I walked back to where I lived. As I approached the house I heard the telephone ringing. I ran to answer it. It was my friend and she told me that she had just received good news from the hospital: her friend had just come out of the coma. Sadly, though, he did later pass away. It was his time.

I asked my psychic friend later whether she could think of any significance in my "seeing" the photograph of the uniformed man and the image of the soaring bird. She told me: "My Native American friend was in the Canadian Air Force during the Second World War. The fact that you immediately picked up his vision in uniform was hardly surprising since he'd suffered great trauma during service—and trauma is often the first thing picked up by psychics, as it leaves strong aural impressions. The flying bird that you saw ... was especially meaningful: not only did it serve to convince me that his soul could not be prevented from flying off, but his wife had also placed a favorite photograph of a flying seagull at his bedside."

On another occasion, a friend told me that his mother had had a massive brain hemorrhage and was in a coma in the hospital. The prognosis was very doubtful as to whether she would recover at all. I told him of my previous experience and asked him if he wanted me to try and concentrate on his mother. He said two words, "Please, Gareth." Over a period of several days I repeated the process that had come naturally to me that first time.

At the end of the week, I called my friend and asked him, somewhat tentatively, about his mother, He told me that a wonderful event had occurred. A nurse who was monitoring his mother had routinely greeted her one morning (as nurses do to coma victims), and to her astonishment heard my friend's mother greet her in return. After this she continued to make a steady recovery, and later was discharged from the hospital and went home.

Now, in both cases, was this coincidence, sheer chance? Perhaps, perhaps not. But allowing myself to believe that my meditations might contribute to healing taking place could at the very least have been positive, not negative.

I believe that we only access a small portion of the true healing power within us, which we can find by beginning to fill and heal ourselves with reconnection to nature, not by consumption and consumerism.

The West African shaman and scholar Malidoma Patrice Somé once wrote that "feelings of absence, of being out of touch, any form of alienation, anonymity and purposelessness—all are symptomatic of a disconnection with the earth."[52] Such feelings result in our attempting to fill the void caused through disconnection by compulsive behavior such as consumption; hence the phenomenon of eating disorders in the West. Instead, we need to reconnect to the earth, to fill ourselves spiritually, to touch the earth and to recognize that we are part of wondrous dynamic whole. Through reconnection, spiritual and physical healing can be found.

Connection is possible, and is not far away from us, as I think this book demonstrates. In this modern age we subconsciously try and attain a connection with the earth. Why else, for example, do we keep plants in our homes, keep pets as companions,[53] drive great distances on the weekends to be in natural surroundings and seek out the sun for our holidays?

We need to take such actions and connections further to *consciously* feel a part of the earth. By so doing, the reward to ourselves will be enormous—as the following words demonstrate:

Come, listen to the Earth with us,
For those who have learned to hear the song,
the earth can soothe the troubled heart,
refresh the weary,
soften the hardened
redirect the lost.

STEVE VAN MATRE—*The Earth Speaks*

I once saw a profound example of a city person connecting with nature. I was in London for a book promotion, and between interviews I went for a walk in one of the many parks. As I walked, I noticed a woman in the distance stepping briskly and businesslike, briefcase in hand, heels clicking on the path. She held her head high and her lips stern.

As we approached each other, I suddenly saw a gray squirrel bounce across the lawn and head directly toward the woman as if it had known her all its life. I watched as then the woman stopped and stared incredulously as the happy little animal bounded up to her. Then there was a transformation. The woman's posture changed dramatically. Her shoulders relaxed, her eyes sparkled and a smile radiated from her face. As I passed, she bent down to the squirrel and peered at it with great joy.

I looked back a little later and saw that the woman was sitting on a bench; she pulled what I presumed was her lunchtime sandwich from her briefcase to share with the little one of a wild free heart in a city of millions of humans. The women had been "earthed" by the squirrel. To me the scene emphasized that whatever the environment, man's contact with what is natural and wild is essential for spiritual uplifting and real attunement to the natural world. It was a delightful, heartening scene that I had witnessed. Connection is possible even in cities.

There was a time when I lived in London for several months. I had left the world of lions in Kenya and was planning to return to South Africa to write a book. I often felt claustrophobic in the city, particularly on those seemingly endless gray days. Whenever I felt very claustrophobic, I would walk to one of the parks and, from a base of a tree, I would reaffirm my connection with nature, with squirrels and birds around me,

This reconnection with nature grows as you repeatedly make a conscious decision to affirm it. As I write this, I do not live in the wilds but in the countryside outside the city of Johannesburg in South Africa. Because my appreciation of nature and my place in it is heightened through a process of continuing to affirm the connection, the sight of a single lizard on my veranda thrills me. I look at it in wonder. I feel the same when birds flutter nearby. I revel in the experience of spotting a raptor flying overhead, and chuckle when I find a porcupine's quill while walking my dogs. These sights and moments make me feel alive. They give me identity. It is a question of allowing yourself to see God in everything and to see all things in nature as members of one whole community, of which you too are a part.

When I do go back into the wilds, where I have spent much of my adult life, I become almost overwhelmed by the beauty of the bush, the majesty of mountains and the serenity of a sunset.

I feel so close to God, and very humble indeed. It is a question of being able to see God in everything, seeing God of all things.

Inspired by the Wild

When you increasingly identify yourself in nature, empathizing and feeling for all life, a wonderful state can be attained. Within a single leaf upon a tree you can see the entire world. The leaf lives and you live and in turn you can feel the leaf's pulsating life, for you yourself know what it is like to be alive. When this state is attained you have reached kinship with all life.

Once you grow close to nature, you become very attuned to the rhythms of life, the seasons and their changes. I became very sensitive to these rhythms of life when I lived with my lions in the Tuli bushlands. The animals, I believe, sense the impending changes of the seasons at a very deep level. Often I lived with the lions in times of great sapping heat, when it seemed that rain would never come again to the land to replenish the earth. Temperatures would rise to as high as 120°F in the shade. But always, just prior to but also just after the arrival of the eventual rains, I would notice a beautiful sign in the kudu antelope herds that the time of hardship was about to come to an end.

I call this sign the gentle "merry-go-round dance of the rains." Suddenly, the once listless kudu would begin to dance around and around, often pretending that they had heard something. They would then "mock-listen" for a few moments before once again dancing around. Upon seeing this delightful sign, I knew that the land was to be rejuvenated. The lions too would become more exuberant just prior to the rains and just after they had fallen. Upon the rains' arrival I would often simply stand outside and let the pelting raindrops drench my body. Like the land around me, the rain would replenish my soul too.

Very few people actually saw me with the lions, but on the rare occasion when I was seen with them the onlookers were always visibly moved. The sight of a lioness running up to me and then leaping up onto her hind legs and embracing me around my bare shoulders touched people very deeply. I think that the sight stirred within them some distant ancestral memory of a "golden age," an age that I believe we subconsciously miss terribly today. It was an age when man was not in conflict with nature but when we embraced nature. It is an age, though, that through reconnection with the earth we can all aspire to in the future. This subconscious memory is, I believe, what stirred people when they saw me with the lions.

Brian Jackman, well-known wildlife journalist and writer of the very successful TV series *The Big Cat Diary*, once saw me among my lions. Early on the morning of the last day of his visit to my camp the lions came to me. I had heard them calling at dawn, and in response I had called back to them. Leaving Brian behind the camp fence, I stepped through the gate to await the lions' arrival. Rafiki appeared first. This is Brian's own account of what took place: "I could hear the thud of her feet as she ran straight at Gareth, then rose on her hind legs to place her huge front paws over his shoulders, while he in turn hugged her and stroked her tawny flanks. 'Rafiki,' he murmured, and the big lioness grunted with pleasure at seeing her friend again."[54]

Many months later in another part of Botswana, Brian met a good friend of mine. He told her of what he had seen that morning, Rafiki's greeting me, and described it as the most remarkable sight in his thirty-year career as a wildlife writer. "I had tears in my eyes as I watched," Brian told my friend.

Even my detractors, those who criticized my work, have been moved almost to tears upon seeing me with the lions. On one painfully sad occasion, the time when Furaha and the two cubs were falsely accused of killing a man, I stepped out of the vehicle of a critic of mine and walked toward Furaha to be with her one last time. As I left the vehicle, the man said to me, "You're mad! She has just killed a man." He could not comprehend the depth of my bond with the lions.

I called Furaha's name and she called back to me. I stepped up to her, then crouched beside her, wishing that this could be where we could remain, in our private world, in lion life. Julie was also in the man's vehicle. When the man was watching Furaha and me together she looked at him for a slight moment. Julie later told me that the man had looked "strangely moved" by the scene and it seemed that his eyes were about to water.

A good friend of mine wrote the following about the experience of seeing the lions and me together.

> I was one of the few privileged people who was allowed to stay at Tawana camp with Gareth and Julie. Many times I have seen Gareth with the lions and always it was an emotional experience. I knew I was witnessing something extraordinary. I have heard him calling across the Tuli bushlands in the early evening. I have heard the lion responding. I have watched the greeting ceremony where Gareth became part of the pride, where nothing else in the world mattered to him. I have seen the love between man and beast. I will never forget it.

With the lions there was much joy, but also great sadness and the most tragic times. But the good and the bad ultimately took place for the purpose of a symbolic message.

Today, unlike in the past, I understand this. It is the message that with love and empathy man can overcome the myth of the "species barrier" and can embrace the "other" in nature—that we can all identify ourselves in nature and can, in doing so, find true spiritual fulfillment. In my own case it leaves me confident in the knowledge that, just as I walked with the lions physically, spiritually I continue to walk with them. Nothing, after all, can erase that spiritual energy and the memory that I believe has become part of me and perhaps also part of the land we lived in, forever.

Letting Go of Anger

Once I held great anger, an anger that bordered on hatred. This was due to many factors, but primarily to the human actions I had witnessed upon animals. Over many long years I saw many fatal casualties of poaching, trophy hunting and the lack of protection and of compassion for wildlife afforded by humans. Lions that I had known so well were slaughtered. Beautiful beings were reduced to bones and rotting flesh while others were transformed into stiff, lifeless facsimiles of their living selves—mounted trophies for what are probably very insecure men. I witnessed elephants riddled with bullets but still standing and alive, incensed to the point of insanity with pain. I witnessed lions with poachers' snares embedded deep within their necks. Once I even had to put the killing bullet into an elephant's brain to release it from the immense pain of the suffering of a rotten leg caused by a poacher's snare that was embedded to the bone. I have witnessed the sight of slumped dead elephants many times, their heads hacked open by man for their tusks.

Great anger, born of my witnessing so much suffering and death, bubbled within me, sometimes spilling out of me and causing me to lash out irrationally. That anger ate away at my soul, leaving me spiritually poorer. Very gradually, though, I began to realize that this great anger was very detrimental to my physical well-being and to my spiritual growth. Bit by bit, I learned to let go of the anger, and mercifully it has almost entirely left me. Today, I try not to allow anger to enter and eat me. It has been an immensely liberating process, freeing myself from anger. I am no longer a slave to that negative emotion called "great anger."

Great anger is such a strange emotion. It does us no good, yet we often hold on to it almost as if it is a medal or badge awarded to us because we were hurt. We have difficulty letting go of anger. Why? We hold on to the great anger for, in a strange way, we feel it empowers us in this isolated world. "I have the right to be angry," we tell ourselves and others around us. We cling to the great anger for it gives us an opportunity to be heard, to make a point, to add to our identity somehow.

The truth is that we do not need great anger as a part of our personality to feel important or to be empowered. First, we are all important, and second, holding on to great anger enslaves us. This anger saps us emotionally and spiritually. By letting go of the anger and identifying the lessons to be learned in our hurt, growth and self-liberation can be found. And here meditation again can help enormously.

Try doing the following each morning and each evening when you feel anger and hurt.

1. Still yourself and do the breathing exercises as instructed in the previous meditations.

2. Once stilled and relaxed, visualize, as you breathe out, your anger leaving your inner being.

3. Breathe out all of your anger. Let the anger go. Visualize the harmful anger leaving you, and say to yourself: "I am letting go of anger so that I can be free. I am letting go of anger to release the past." You are cleansing yourself.

When in time you feel that you have rid yourself of much of the anger (and this will be a gradual process) you can move forward to try to project what I called the "light of goodness" onto those who have hurt you.

After I let go of my anger, I began to learn to project this light onto those who perceived themselves as my enemies. I "throw" light onto them instead of hating them. I came to understand that these people's wrongful actions are probably manifestations of great harm done to them sometime in their lives. I learned that by hating, I was not healing. I was not healing myself or the person who had caused my hurt.

Today when I feel hurt, after releasing my anger, I visualize this "light of goodness" upon the person who causes my hurt. Hatred and anger cannot change bad actions but at least, by giving light, the possibility exists that you could be helping to release from the hurtful one the pain that causes them to act in the hurtful way.

I know that this might sound a strange concept, but I believe in it and encourage you to try this process whenever someone affects you negatively. I am not asking you to love your enemy, but just to give light to them. At first it will not be easy because of the anger within you. But as you learn to let go of the anger, the process will become easier.

1. Relax and breathe as instructed in the previous meditations.

2. Visualize the person who has hurt you.

3. See their body, their form, being illuminated with the light of goodness.

4. Concentrate upon this image for several minutes.

With practice you will learn to project the light in everyday life—while, say, you are in your office. Let go of hate and anger, release the chains of the past and try to project the light of goodness. In turn, you might be pleasantly surprised in the change of behavior in the one that hurt you.

Try to always remember that "Life is too short and too wonderful. There is no time to be unkind (hateful) or envious ... for you can be equal to the greatness of life only by marching with it, not by seeking love but by giving it, not seeking to be understood but learning to understand."[55]

On Life after Life

The loss of a loved one, and particularly the loss of one's own child, is perhaps the deepest grief a person can feel. When I lost

Batian I experienced such grief. But after a wondrous experience one day near his grave, I began to learn, gradually, how to deal with grief and to understand death more fully. That experience was a gift, a lesson from Batian. I recount it here in the hope that it might help and comfort someone confronted with the death of a loved one.

On the second anniversary of Batian's death I walked to where I had buried him, beneath a cairn of beautiful stones. There the experience was about to take place, a clear signpost that Batian was still with me, that he lives on in spirit and that it was time to let go of sadness.

To explain the experience fully, I must first regress to the time shortly after Batian was killed. After I buried his remains I took an identification collar (which I had put on him for a time) down to the grave and placed it in a hole in a tree near the cairn of stones.

On the first anniversary of his death I went to the grave and put my hand into the hole, expecting to feel the collar. To my surprise I found that it was empty. I then thought that perhaps an elephant with its curious, reaching trunk had found the collar in the hole, pulled it out and dropped it somewhere nearby. I searched thoroughly in the nearby bush but did not find it.

A year later, on the second anniversary of his death, I stood beside the grave on a bright morning before moving away to sit beneath the tree in which I had put the collar. Sitting there, I began to visualize what Batian would have looked like had he still been alive. He would have been five years old; he had been big for his age and I believe he would have grown into one of the largest lions ever to range the Tuli bushlands. As I sat there, I willed that I could receive some sign from him. After a while I stood and walked back toward the cairn of stones. Suddenly, upon the dusty ground, I saw the fresh paw prints of a lion. I had walked on that same piece of ground earlier but had seen no lion tracks. It is impossible that I could have missed them.

In the bush one reads the ground like a newspaper and one's life can depend on what it tells one. The size of the paw prints were the same as Batian's before he was killed.

I took a big breath in an attempt to calm myself and recover from the shock of seeing the tracks, then began to follow where the paw prints led. Incredibly, the tracks led me directly to the cairn of stones and then onward. I continued to follow the tracks—then suddenly saw Batian's identification collar directly where the paw prints were leading. I had received my sign from him.

The last time I had seen the collar it had been buckled to form a circle. But that morning, when I had found it, it lay stretched out upon the ground. It had not been unbuckled but somehow had been cut.

I picked up the collar, held it to my chest and spoke to Batian. Then I returned to the tree and once again placed the collar in the hole. Afterwards, filled with feelings of elation coupled with shock, I made my way through the hills and the valleys, back to my camp.

In the days to come I pondered much on the experience, on how the tracks seemingly just materialized and how they led me to find Batian's long-lost collar. I also pondered on the symbolism of the collar being cut and how it was laid out straight upon the ground.

Today, I firmly believe that Batian was showing me that he lives on in spirit, and by leading me to the cut collar was leading me to the understanding that I should make a break from my grief (hence the collar being cut and laid straight out upon the ground). To this day, the experience is very comforting to me. Every day I know that my beloved Batian is never too far away from me.

In all that lives around us our loved ones who have passed over watch us, care for us and I believe can present signposts in our lives to help guide us on the path that we walk on earth.

A beautiful poem by Frances Nnaggenda sums up my own feelings about where our loved ones go when they die. They remain a part of us and a part of everything around us.

> The dead are not under the earth
> They are in the tree that rustles
> They are in the woods that groan
> They are in the water that runs
> They are in the hut, they are in the crowd
> The dead are not dead
> Those who are dead are never gone
> They are in the breast of a woman
> They are in the child that is wailing and in the fire
>   that flames
> The dead are not under the earth
> They are in the fire that is dying
> They are in the grass that is weeping
> They are in the whimpering rocks
> They are in the forest, they are in the house
> They are not dead.

CHAPTER 5

Lion Power!
The Seven Vital
Precepts of the Lion

Part I:

Infusing & Enhancing Your Life
with Lion Power!

As already illustrated in this book, the lion was a great symbol of divinity and guardianship to our ancestors. In these modern times we have lost our connection with the lion and also, by no coincidence, lost our understanding of our place in nature. We have become separated from the whole, a lonely species.

Today, though, people worldwide are realizing that we have become disconnected and that, separate from nature and even separate from each other, we cannot possibly experience life to the full. Hence there is an enormous need to rediscover and to enhance within ourselves principles which can reconnect us to the whole and which can blossom within us true spiritual fulfillment.

Drawing from the essence of what George Adamson once wrote about the precepts, the principles, of the lion, I was inspired, in turn, to conceptualize how we can all begin to reconnect and to enhance our lives.

George wrote: "Self-reliance and courage, tenacious yet realistic defense of a realm, the willingness to care for the young of another, brotherhood, loyalty and affection are seven commendable precepts ... their [the lions'] code of behavior is worth our respect."[56]

Self-reliance, fellowship, willingness to care, affection, determination, courage and loyalty. These, adapted from George's in-
sight, are to me the seven vital precepts of the lion. They are
"vital" in the sense that they are intensely strong and energized
codes of behavior, codes that are the central tenets of lion society.

The lions roaming the last wild lands of Africa hold enormous freedom in their hearts. They are born free and live with
vitality. They cannot be enslaved. How many of us in this modern
world can claim to be like the lions, truly free, vital and un-
shackled? Living as intimately as I did among lions and witnessing the lions' precepts on a daily basis, I began to realize that
we have much to learn and gain from the lion. I began to realize
that if we can infuse our psyche with the lions' seven main precepts, we can discard the chains of our fears ... and that we too
can hold great freedom in our hearts.

I truly believe that the seven precepts of the lion can be
heightened within each and every one of us. If we wish to infuse
our psyche with these precepts, I believe that they can contribute
to our living our lives more fully and more positively, turn dreams
into reality and assist us to find and fulfill our purpose in life.
And we all have a purpose, for why else would we exist? To
exist is to have purpose.

In this chapter and the next are seven sections containing
stories of the seven precepts as I and others have witnessed them.
At the end of each of the seven sections there is a description of
a scene that embodies the essence of the particular precept.
This is the meditation/visualization scene.

To heighten within yourself the power of the precepts, attempt
the following exercise at the end of each of the sections.

1. Go to a peaceful place, preferably outside (perhaps in a
   field or park) but otherwise in a sanctuary, for example
   your bedroom (if indoors, play a relaxation tape or CD).

2. Sit down in a comfortable position, close your eyes and begin to relax. Breathe in slowly, hold your breath for two seconds, then breathe out. Try to continue to breathe like this throughout the session.

3. As you begin to relax, feel yourself becoming connected with the earth. Beginning with your head, then neck and shoulders, feel yourself drawn downward and toward being "connected." Become grounded and feel a part of our beautiful earth.

4. After several minutes, when you feel relaxed and at peace, begin to visualize the particular meditation/visualization scene. Feel its meaning and draw inspiration from it. Breathe in, hold your breath for two seconds, visualize the scene, then breathe out.

5. Do this for several more minutes. Feel the power of the precept. Feel Lion Power!

The heightened precept power will come to you with practice and continued meditation time. Heightened self-reliance, fellowship, willingness to care, affection, determination, courage, and loyalty are attainable for everyone. With continued meditation and visualization they become stronger and stronger. It is a gift to be cherished from nature.

Precepts Sessions

Lion Power! Precept One
DARKY, A STORY OF SELF-RELIANCE

It was a profound experience to know Darky, the Lion King of the Tuli bushlands. I first encountered this magnificent lion in 1983 and knew him for almost a decade. He was a great, stately gray lion with a full dark mane. I view Darky as my "lion father," for he taught me much about his kind. He also taught me about self-reliance. His life and his capability to overcome adversity embodied great self-reliance.

Darky was an almost mystical lion. At times I thought that immortals did exist, and that Darky was one of them. His state, his being, remained so constant in the bushlands that it seemed he could have lived there forever. Darky was the bushlands.

Whenever I think of Darky, I see in my mind a male lion resting alone upon a rise on the plains. I see Darky looking out upon all that he was a part of. Alone, yet a part of. The scene is one. The plains would not be the plains without him, and he would not be he without the plains.

In 1983, Darky was one of the two "Lords" of the Lower Majale, an ancestral lion territory in the Southern Tuli Bushlands. Kgosi[57] was the elder of the two pride males, a stately and proud lion who exuded unleashed power and might. Kgosi's mane was spectacular and flowed like a murky river across his tawny back, down beneath his chest and tapering toward his belly.

Kgosi and Darky resting together on the plains was an inspiring sight, and at night their great territorial calls would float across the land like a cosmic wave. Upon hearing them I would always be filled with a sense of well-being: at times I would raise my hand in the direction of their leonine song and feel a part of their energy.

At its height, the Lower Majale pride consisted of nineteen lions; the two pride males, six beautiful lionesses and eleven tumbling cubs. Darky was a particularly tolerant father. The cubs loved to play on his reclining body and to swat at his twitching tail. He would groan softly as the cubs jumped upon his shaggy head and back. Eventually, when the cubs' games became over-boisterous, he would raise his upper lip and give a short snarl. At this, they would scatter away back to their mothers. This, though, was all part of the game as they would inevitably return, stalk him, then jump on him. Then, equally inevitably, he would eventually snarl again, the cubs would scatter ... and the pantomime would continue until, with the setting sun, the entire pride (after much stretching and yawning) moved away into the night.

Tragically, within two years of my knowing the lions, Darky's pride was severely fractured by the actions of hunters and poachers. One day Kgosi and two lionesses found themselves on the game farms beyond the boundaries of the Tuli. It was very likely that trophy hunters with baits had lured them out. I never saw Kgosi or the two lionesses again. They were shot dead by white hunters, men who think it is manly and heroic to kill the King of Beasts. The sound of gunfire beyond the Tuli boundaries signified the destruction of the brotherhood of Kgosi and Darky.

Darky was now the lone pride protector, and single pride males are normally vulnerable to the incursions of younger, no-madic males, eager to oust the old and to take over a pride. Amaz-ingly though, Darky, the self-reliant, went on to rule alone over the Lower Majale for another eight long years.[58] Over those years, his foes were not only young challenging males, but also the white hunters beyond the reserve's boundary. In fact they posed the greatest danger; they knew well of his existence and some sorely sought the opportunity to kill him as the ultimate lion trophy. They referred to Darky as the "Big Black Mane" or the "Swart Een," the "Black One." In bushveld bars and around campfires they would speak of a legendary Botswana lion of great size, fierceness and cunning. They spoke of him in such terms because they always failed to kill him. Darky outwitted them instead and belittled them. Some thought him to be somehow "pro-tected." The truth is, he was protected; he lived as long as he did for a purpose, a portion of which, I believe, was to teach and inspire me. Darky defied the white hunters and their guns, the poachers with their traps and the challenges of pride takeovers by the wandering nomadic male lions.

Once, two adult male lions left their territory in the north and headed into the fringe areas of Darky's range. A confrontation was inevitable and when it took place the sounds of a great battle echoed off the hills and through the valleys. And Darky emerged victorious.

At the site of the battle, upon the scarred and defaced ground, a large tuft of thick black mane was found. Embedded within the fur was the sheath of a hooked claw.

After the battle, I set out in search of Darky. I feared that he might have sustained terrible injuries. Late in the afternoon, I found the great old warrior upon his rise on the Pitsani plains. At my approach, although clearly weary and torn, he only exuded calmness to me. As evening closed in, I left my friend and that night raised my hand as I heard his haunting calls flowing through the air from across the plains.

Three years after first knowing Darky, I left the Tuli bushlands. I left because I knew that I had to concentrate on completing (and finding a publisher for) the book that I had been writing about the Tuli lions and their plight. I left because I knew that I could not motivate the authorities from within the bushlands to better protect Darky and his kind. Therefore, I had decided that I would attempt to motivate awareness for the Tuli lions' greater protection externally—through having my book published.

During those three years, I had had the privilege of learning much about the African lion. I had also moved forward in myself. The lions had fueled me forward.

Looking back today, I see that stage of my life as being my "young adult lion" stage and somehow Darky, my lion father, just prior to my leaving the bushlands, recognized this in me.

Upon entering young adulthood, young male lions are usually ousted from the pride and its security by the pride males. It is as if they are chased away toward their own self-discovery of self-reliance. When this time comes, the young princes have to walk alone to learn self-reliance and to be aware of intuition, for their lives depend upon it. In time, a young prince will form an alliance with another male (or males). These alliances, if strong and well bonded, then lead to the princes becoming kings as they then challenge pride males. With the ousting of the old, the new kings become the pride's new protectors, siring their own sons and daughters until their own day comes ... and they have to return to the world of self-reliance.

Now, during those three years of growing in the bushlands, Darky had not once, ever, shown anger toward me—regardless of whether I was in a vehicle when I encountered him, or on foot. Then one day, just prior to my leaving the bushlands, in the very core, the very heartland of his territory, Darky sought to chase me out of his land. It was as though he knew, as he recognized with his own sons, it was time for me to undertake the big walk, to travel to distant places, to learn externally and internally.

His ousting me from his territory was dramatic and moving. During and just after the incident, not understanding, I called to him, "Why, Darky?" I did not comprehend why he had acted toward me as he did. Sometime afterwards, though, I began to understand. It was my time to go, he had told me—and this had coincided almost exactly with the time of my own inner decision to leave the bushlands. The incident happened just after having made that decision and today I understand that it occurred to affirm my decision.

The incident took place one morning as I was tracking Darky on foot. My intuition that morning told me strongly to beware. I felt a foreboding of danger that I had never felt before while tracking him. I followed his tracks through thick undergrowth, then onto a wide and open flood plain. Then it happened.

Branches cracked and splintered. I swung around, and saw Darky crashing toward me in great bounds. "No, Darky!" I shouted. He came from the thicket, fast and low—a blur of charcoal and tawny. I shouted at him again and he stopped, crouching upon his tracks. I walked backward, attempting to open the distance between us, to show him that I was moving away from his core area. Then suddenly he bounded forward again in great heavy rushes. In a flash, it seemed that the distance between us was being eaten up. Forty meters became twenty. I loaded my rifle and fired a shot over his head, praying that a warning shot would turn him away. Darky then spun in the air and bounded away into the heavy undergrowth.

I breathed out and walked away, with a feeling that merged bewilderment, anger and sorrow. As I mentioned previously, today I understand that this incident was an affirmation that it was indeed time to leave the Tuli. It was, of course, the right decision. Like a young adult lion, upon leaving I wandered far and wide on my lion path. I traveled from the Indian Ocean through forests and deserts to the opposite side of southern Africa, where the Atlantic breakers crash upon desert sands. I traveled north and met "Baba ya Simba," the Father of the Lions—George Adamson.

As I walked away from the flood plain that day, I could never have imagined that I would return two-and-a-half years later, and that my role would be to guide three young lions toward their own self-reliance and independence. No, when I left the bushlands, I simply wondered if I would ever see Darky again....

And see him again I certainly did!

Upon my return to the Tuli bushlands toward the end of 1989, it was with immense delight that I learned that Darky was alive and still very much the King of the Lower Majale. Later, though, I was alarmed to learn how a year before he had been caught by a poacher's snare. The lasso of death around his neck should have killed him as the snares have killed so many Tuli lions over the years. Unbelievably, though, he had survived. Darky had fought the snare and, by biting down hard upon the cable wire, freed himself. It was an extraordinary feat of strength and courage but resulted in his snapping two of his incisor teeth. This loss should have limited him while hunting, but amazingly it did not. Darky continued to hunt successfully for himself, at times even pulling down full-grown eland bulls (Africa's largest antelope), which would have weighed almost a ton, alone.

During the early part of the rehabilitation of George's young lions, Darky occasionally trekked north to my camp, which was situated beyond his territory. During that stage of the rehabilitation project George's lions were too young and vulnerable to be out in the wilds at night, and I kept them in what I called the "cubs' enclosure," a fenced-off area that was part of the overall camp.

At night, on several occasions, Darky came right up to the fence of the cubs' enclosure and stood there, staring in at the youngsters (who were obviously greatly intimidated by the presence of the old warrior). Darky did not show any aggression toward the youngsters on these occasions; he was calm and seemingly just curious. At times I did fear that in the months ahead he might harass the youngsters as the rehabilitation progressed—but this did not occur. As my lions grew and became increasingly territorial, Darky seemingly respected their claims to this land north of his territory.

Two years later, with my lions now settled well into the bushlands, both my lion father and my lion son (Batian) were lost to me. In a single week, Darky disappeared and Batian was killed. Batian had just reached the stage where he was challenging the old pride male for dominance over the Lower Majale pride. There was a confrontation between the two males, and signs of the battle on the ground—masses of black mane, indicating that Darky had been toppled from his throne.

Just days after this confrontation, Batian, together with several of the Lower Majale lionesses, was lured out of the Tuli bushlands by hunters. On a hunting farm my Batian was murdered. Murdered too, within the same week, were two of the lionesses.

From the night of the confrontation with Batian, Darky was never seen again in the Lower Majale territory. It was presumed by many that the old lion had succumbed to his wounds and died in a quiet place where he had roamed and ruled for so long. The following words describe a lion's dignity and inner strength even when death calls:

> He was found lying in the grass beneath a tree near the Masaal Kopjes. Some disease must have prevented him from hunting, for he was now only a skeleton held together by slack hide. But his large brown mane attested to his former glory. He reclined on his side, too weak to raise his head, only his eyes showing of the final tenacity with which he clung to life. At dusk, he heard distant roars and, with a last effort, he grunted weakly several times, trying to retain a vestige of contact with the community of which he had been a part. That night death came to him as he lay calmly alone beneath his tree.[59]

February 1994, three years after Batian's death and the disappearance (and what was thought to be the almost certain death) of Darky, I was told a story that was strange and, at the same time, alarming. While visiting the Tuli, a Motswana friend of mine told me that an old black-maned lion, resembling Darky, was killing livestock near a village some sixty kilometers from the bushlands. My friend also told me that people were trying to hunt the lion down.

"Could this really be Darky, still alive?" I asked myself. I was determined that I would search for the lion and, if successful, have him tranquilized and moved back into the bushlands. The thought of my lion father dying, bullet-ridden, as a cattle killer was too much to bear. I then set out toward the village, a two-hour drive over rutted tracks.

At the village I learned more about the lion from friends and the local police. Some people who knew Darky and had seen the cattle-killing lion were convinced it was the same lion. I was also told of how a group of vengeful cattle owners had set out in search of the old black-maned lion just two days previously. They had tracked him, then found him sitting calmly at the bottom of a hill.

Upon seeing him, two of the men told the others that the lion ahead of them was Darky. (Darky had been well known and respected for years by the people of the Tuli.) One member of the party disagreed and said that he was going to move forward. He took aim, fired and missed. Darky just sat there, unmoving, but now staring intently in the direction from which the shot had come. The man fired again, this time too high. The bullet hit the hillside and Darky turned his head to where the bullet had struck. Darky then stood up and slowly stepped in the direction of the shooter. At this, the man hurried back to the others and there was a short discussion, whereupon it was agreed that the lion was Darky and the party fled from the scene.

For over a week I covered hundreds of square kilometers searching but finding only elusive signs of Darky's passage. I gained information about his movements from the people living at isolated cattle posts and eventually my search led me increasingly toward the northern boundary of the Tuli bushlands.

One evening, I knew I was close to him. I felt his presence and was relieved that he was heading toward the protected area. Late the following afternoon my search brought me to the vicinity of the fence that divides the Tuli bushlands from the cattle country. There I found the tracks of a male lion and they led me up to the boundary fence. I then saw where a lion had crawled underneath the fence. Several long, dark mane hairs were caught on the bottom strand of wire.

The old man had made it safely back to the land where he was born.

Darky's life was not filled with inner fears. He was a wonderful symbol of self-reliance. He embodied courage, calmness and self-freedom. A great lesson to draw from Darky's life is that we too should hold freedom in our hearts. We should never allow society to steal this freedom from us. Let go of your fears and fuel yourself with Darky's courage to enable you to do this. Hold on to freedom and let go of the fear of failure.

Meditation/Visualization Scene
SELF-RELIANCE

1. Go to your peaceful place (if indoors, put on a relaxation tape/CD of soothing music).

2. Sit down in a comfortable position, close your eyes and begin to relax. Breathe in slowly, hold your breath for two seconds and then breathe out. Try to continue to breathe like this throughout this session.

3. As you begin to relax, feel yourself becoming connected to the earth. Beginning with your head, then neck and shoulders, feel yourself drawn downward to the earth.

4. After several minutes, when you feel relaxed and at peace, visualize Darky sitting upon a rise on the plain. He calmly looks out over all of which he is a part. Darky is the symbol of self-reliance. He holds no fears. Draw such self-reliance within yourself. Feel self-reliance growing within yourself ... feel strong.

5. Darky's view from the rise is beautiful....

6. Do this for several minutes. Feel the power of the precept.

Lion Power! Precept Two
FELLOWSHIP—ON BEING LINKED BY SOUL

A pride of lions is "fellowship." It is as simple as that. My personal dictionary's definition of fellowship would be "a lion's pride." Like wolves, lions live in social groupings and are social beings who blend affection and courage to produce an integrated communal system, with each pride member having a purpose.

Today, in contrast, in mankind's modern Western world, our social system has been inflicted by disintegrating family values. Sense of community, the sense of the original and universal "Ubuntu," the understanding that "I am, because we are, and since we are, therefore I am": these are the values we are losing. And we are left poorer. But with regards to fellowship and community, we have the opportunity to learn much from the lion (and the wolf).

The lions live in a way that enforces the family with strength and unity. When food is obtained, even the sick and the old have the opportunity to eat. The lions' education of their young is a long process lasting at least eighteen months. The lion family, united by fellowship, defends its territory with a blend of tenacity and realism.

Today we should learn from the lion and inject fellowship again into our own community. We can be strong as individuals and yet put a portion of ourselves into the overall good of the family and direct community. Visualize becoming integrated into the community like a member of a lion pride—individual, yet part of the whole, and having purpose to it all.

There are a few of us humans who have had the great privilege of sharing lion fellowship. With my lions in the Tuli bushlands, I was embraced by and in turn embraced that fellowship. It is very strong, lion fellowship. A unity of souls. George Adamson, of course, experienced great lion fellowship. In fact he embodied its very meaning, and to his very last day he held this heightened fellowship. Such heightened fellowship is personally incredibly enriching and enhances the lives of everyone around you. Once you attain it, you will in turn radiate it.

Let me tell you some stories about heightened fellowship. Of Adamson and his lions I could write many, but there is one story that is particularly poignant and inspiring. The night of the final filming day of the last documentary to be made on George's life found us, the film team, George and friends, relaxing at Kampi ya Simba with song, drinks, fellowship and happiness. The night sky was the deepest inky indigo, punctured by the stars like piercing diamonds. Jerry, an Irish priest friend of George's, was playing the guitar and singing beautifully. The lions, the wild pride of Growe and the others, were somewhere out there in the vast dark bushlands.

At the end of one song, George suddenly asked, "Jerry, do you know the Irish song 'Mountains of Mourne?'" Jerry replied, "I do, George, I do," and began to play. At this, George began to sing. Just as he had sung the very first words, a terrific chorus of lion calls reverberated through the wilds and echoed off the nearby Kora Rock, shadowed by the night. The lions were very close by and had responded with strength and unity upon hearing the old pride master's voice. George did not falter for a second and sang on, as his pride replied repeatedly in unison. It was simply wonderful and magical. The old man was one of them, part of the pride, and together the man and the lions rejoiced in their fellowship. Among my many marvelous memories of Kora, George and his lions, this was singularly the most stirring.

In time at Kora, Growe and her pride began to know me. I tracked them daily during the filming period and a fellowship developed between us. One evening I stopped to spend the night upon the great granite Kaume Hills that overlook the Tana River, Kenya's largest river. I knew that Growe and her pride were close by, as I had tracked them for much of the day. That night the lions came to where I was with the Land Rover and I felt as though the lions and I were being drawn to each other. Instead of approaching me silently, they called to me softly as they drifted down the side of the hill in the moonlight. A sense of great calm prevailed as they came toward the slab of rock upon which I stood. It was magical.

I slept on the roof of George's battered old Land Rover (the one in which he was murdered almost a year later). At times during the night I woke up and saw the lions resting nearby, occasionally calling softly to one another. I felt as though I was at one with them, part of the same fellowship. I felt no fears, only a completeness of being among them. When you feel such heightened fellowship, you feel the utter calmness of the spiritual link.

As I have mentioned, there are only a few humans in this modern age that have been blessed by the fellowship of lions. One of those who have had this privilege is my friend Kobie Kruger. In fact, she and all her family felt this fellowship.

Kobie lived with her husband, Kobus, in the Kruger National Park in South Africa, where Kobus was a senior game ranger. One day, Kobus brought home a tiny male cub, and from that moment their lives became touched by a lion. His mother was thought to have been killed by farmers on the park's boundary. The Kruger family cared for the cub, whom they named Leo.

The cub grew into a fine young lion and was almost eighteen months old when I first met him. Leo had a unique relationship with each member of the Kruger family. Kobus was respected and loved as the pride's male; Kobie was Leo's mother, upon whom he trusted and depended for motherly love; Karin, one of the Krugers' three young adult daughters, was Leo's favorite sister, and together they enjoyed much boisterous fun; and Sandra was the sister for whom Leo held the most respect. He understood her quiet, determined ways.

Leo's other human sister was Hettie, a wilderness girl of a passionate nature, who suffered from extreme moods. Leo was extremely perceptive to her feelings. When Hettie was exuberant with light, Leo would become a tawny clown, but when she was wistful he would lie beside her and call softly to her or lick her arms and face to comfort her.

The other member of Leo's "pride" was the Kruger's Australian cattle dog, Wolfie. Leo respected Wolfie enormously.

Even when Leo weighed a hundred kilograms more than Wolfie
did, he still regarded Wolfie as his respected senior.

When I visited the Krugers and Leo for the first time, there
was that soul link connection between the lion and myself. I felt
that connection during the first walk in the bush together. He
demonstrated the connection by stopping and repeatedly licking
my hand. The Krugers were astonished when they saw this as,
apart from the family, they had never seen Leo acting like this with
another person before. It seems that an indescribable recognition takes place between lions and me when they need my help.

The Krugers and I hoped I would be allowed to return Leo
to the wilds in a private conservancy in Zimbabwe. Sadly, permission was not forthcoming, but eventually the Krugers found a
sanctuary situation where Leo could live in the semi-wilds with
others of his kind. It was the best life that they could offer him,
but their parting was terribly sad, for Leo and for the Krugers.

A year later the Kruger family returned to the sanctuary to
visit their lion son. By this time Leo was approaching three years
old. He was a young prince, and he lived in a spacious enclosure
within bush environs with two adult lionesses.

A year is a long time in the life of a lion of only three years.
What would be his reaction when he saw the family again? Would
he be so integrated into life with his own kind that he would
have lost and forgotten his fellowship with the Krugers? These
questions were answered when the family, in great anticipation,
were driven into the sanctuary.

They called his name and Leo soon appeared, looking ques-
tioningly in their direction. Kobus then stepped out of the vehicle
and called to him. Then a wondrous thing happened. To borrow
Kobie's words, "Leo's eyes came alive with a surge of recognition and, calling deeply, he rushed toward Kobus, throwing his
body against him in affection!" Kobie was shaking with pure joy
as she watched Kobus and Leo together. Then she and Karin also
stepped out of the vehicle, and when Leo saw them his eyes again

surged with recognition and joy and he rushed up to them. Kobie threw her arms around Leo, and they rubbed cheeks, heads and shoulders. Her tears fell upon his fur. Leo greeted Karin in exactly the same way. I have seen photographs of this great greeting of souls—fellowship. The photographs are incredibly moving, and exude great expressions of love between them all.

Meditation/Visualization Scene
FELLOWSHIP

1. Go to your peaceful place (remember, if indoors, play a relaxation tape/CD of soothing music).

2. Sit down in a comfortable position, close your eyes and begin to relax. Breathe in slowly, hold your breath for two seconds, then breathe out. Try to continue to breathe like this throughout the session.

3. As you begin to relax, feel yourself becoming connected with the earth. Beginning with your head, then neck and shoulders, feel yourself drawn downward to the earth.

4. After several minutes, when you feel relaxed and at peace, visualize the scene of the Kruger family reuniting with Leo. Visualize that great greeting, hugging and great joy. Absorb the heightened fellowship that you can see. Let the fellowship with your loved ones and your community blossom like that of the lions.

5. Do this for several minutes. Feel the power of the precept.

Lion Power! Precept Three
WILLINGNESS TO CARE

Three years ago I witnessed an astonishing display of lions' willingness to care. It involved two young brothers named Tau and Ngala. At that time, together with several colleagues and a vet, we were relocating these males and two lionesses from a rehabilitation center to Lion Haven, the large natural habitat sanctuary we had established.

At the time of the relocation the lions were living in a fenced-off enclosure, and in order to transport them the seventy kilometers to the sanctuary they had to be tranquilized. We had decided that Karata, the elder of the two lionesses, should be the first to be darted. The vet fired a tranquilizing dart at her. It flew through the air and landed accurately on her rump. She experienced little stress during the several minutes that it took her to fall into a fully comatose state.

Ngala was next to be tranquilized. Once again the vet aimed his tranquilizing gun and pulled the trigger. To my utter surprise, Ngala collapsed to the ground at almost the same moment the dart hit him. It was as though he had been poleaxed. I had never before seen a lion react like that when being tranquilized, and therefore I held fears: normally when lions are darted, they fall into an unconscious state after several minutes, as Karata did. However, the vet reassured me and the others who were looking on that it had been a "fluke shot." The dart needle had somehow entered directly into a vein, hence the almost instantaneous reaction. The intravenous (rather than intramuscular) injection had caused Ngala's reaction to the drug to be dramatically quicker than the norm.

Tau, seeing his brother collapse, became very distressed. He walked up to him and called to him softly. He then smelled his brother's body, and in doing so, saw the tranquilizing dart hooked in Ngala's shoulder. Recognizing in some way that the dart was the cause of Ngala's condition, he seized it with his teeth and pulled it loose, then dropped it to the ground. There was a fairly large contingent of members of the media attending the relocation and there were gasps of surprise at this. These people, for the very first time, had seen and recognized lion compassion, the willingness to care within lion society.

A little later Tau was darted. As the dart hit him, he reacted with a start, then increasingly began to feel the effects of the drug. Then, for the second time within minutes, we witnessed the great bond between the two lion brothers. Tau walked unsteadily, in a semi-drugged state, to where Ngala lay. He then sat down beside his brother and, with one of his paws touching Ngala, fell into unconsciousness. It was a deeply moving scene.

During the weeks ahead, both brothers had to be tranquilized again to receive certain medical attention. And once again the brothers' expression of willingness to care for each other was witnessed. As before, a dart was pulled out and the brothers lay beside each other in unified unconsciousness.

Such observations of lions' great willingness to care are in no way unique. The authors of *When Elephants Weep—the Emotional Lives of Animals*[60] write of how, "In the wild, too, wild animals grieve for their companions ... a lion has been known to remain by the body of another lion that had been shot and killed, licking its fur." Predator researchers in the Botswanan Kalahari Desert learned that when one of the male lions they had been studying was, tragically, shot by a trophy hunter, a young pride male stood by the body as if to protect it. He snarled defiantly and charged repeatedly at the hunters when they tried to approach the body to claim their "trophy."

Eventually the hunters were only successful in chasing the younger male away by firing their guns in the air and by driving their vehicles toward him.[61]

This section of the book deals mainly with heightened codes of behavior in the lion, but such precepts are not, of course, restricted to lions alone. I believe that similar precepts exist in all social animals (and other animals too). I saw, for example, strong willingness to care by zebras on two separate touching occasions. The first took place when I was studying the Tuli lion population during a crippling drought in 1983. Early one morning, my tracker, whose name was Fish, and I followed the tracks of the Lalapanzi pride. We entered fairly thick bush and suddenly came across the lions. The pride of sixteen had just pulled down an adult zebra in a dry riverbed below where we were standing. Upon seeing us, the lions dashed away. Inwardly, I cursed myself for having been the cause of their flight.

We then decided to hide nearby in the hope that the lions would return to their kill. We had sat silently in thick bush for over half an hour when, to our amazement, we saw, not the lions, but a small herd of emaciated zebras moving toward the kill. The drought had hit all Tuli zebras extremely hard and this herd was no exception. They plodded forward slowly, dust rising from their hooves. Their once upright manes hung loosely along the napes of their necks.

Despite the scent of the lions upon the ground, the herd walked directly up to the dead zebra. Fish and I watched in amazement as one mare rubbed her muzzle over the dead one's head, then repeatedly pushed it upwards. Each time, it solemnly, and with sad finality, fell back lifelessly onto the parched ground.

The dead zebra had obviously been a part of the herd, a family member, a friend, and the mare obviously had a special attachment to the fallen one. The zebras cared. Eventually the zebra herd moved away, walking slowly down the dry riverbed, perhaps with memories of the fallen one in their minds as they faced their own doubtful future during that time of devastating drought.

The second occasion that I witnessed willingness to care by zebras occurred in the Etosha National Park in Namibia in 1989. Early one morning I came across the body of a female zebra upon the plains. She had recently died, perhaps as a result of snakebite for there were no predators nearby. Beside her fallen body stood her young foal. During the initial hour, as I watched the tragic scene, jackals appeared and began to nose hungrily around the corpse.

As the number of jackals grew, I saw the foal moving directly toward them, attempting to chase them from its mother. I left the sad scene but returned again several hours later. By this time, the blue sky was pinpricked with soaring vultures. Many descended and formed an untidy circle around the mother zebra's body. The foal stood nearby. As time passed, some of the jackals fed on the eyes and pulled at the muzzle of the zebra mother, as whitebacked vultures attacked the nether regions. Then, as I watched the scene, I saw the foal again moving toward its mother's body. It was deliberately attempting to disturb the feasting scavengers. The brave foal's inner feelings were almost tangible that day upon the plains.

I returned to the scene once more in the late afternoon. The foal still stood nearby. By this time as many as sixty vultures were crowding around the corpse. The foal had now remained near its mother's body for at least nine hours, never moving more than forty paces from where the body was being consumed. Once again, as I watched, and as it had done repeatedly throughout the day, the zebra foal walked up to the vultures. This disrupted them and the foal then walked in a circle around the hissing leaping birds. By the day's end the jackals had gathered in large numbers, and as the sun lowered I saw the foal walk up to them and flick its small hooves at them as they moved like great hairy ants around its legs.

Even when lions approached, still the little foal was reluctant to leave its mother. As a pride gathered, the zebra foal even seemingly attempted to disturb the lions on three occasions by walking toward them. One male lion made a halfhearted move toward the foal, and only then did the foal finally move away from what remained of its mother.

This incident was a poignant example of a young zebra's willingness to care, of a compassion that remained unbroken even when tested by flocks of vultures and hordes of jackals: only when faced by lions did the small foal move away ...

The story of Joy Adamson and a lion cub named Kula tells of a double episode of willingness to care.[62] First, we witness joy caring for a small lion cub found alone in the bush and, second, at the story's end, we witness the cub's mother caring for the little one despite their having been apart for almost three weeks.

At the time of this story, Joy was rehabilitating the female leopard named Penny in the Shaba National Reserve in Kenya. The lion cub, Kula (short for Chakula—"food" in Swahili), had been found by a game ranger and the reserve warden had brought the cub to Joy to care for.

During the days that followed, as Joy reared the cub, initially feeding him every two-and-a-half hours, she began to ponder what his future would be. Her darkest fear was that he would be destined for lifelong captivity in a zoo if an alternative could not be found. Joy decided to attempt to locate Kula's mother and, if successful, reunite him with his family.

The pride was indeed found one day. As Joy had planned, the warden drove his vehicle between the pride and her vehicle to shield her as Kula was lifted to the ground in a box. However, it was late in the day, and because of the lack of light the warden thought it best that they postpone Kula's release for another day.

Kula's box was lifted from the ground, but as the ranger did this Kula's mother suddenly appeared from behind a bush and stared intently at the box. The lioness even walked a few steps toward it. Upon seeing this, Joy asked the ranger to replace the box on the ground and to open its door. This done, they moved their vehicles back some thirty meters to monitor what transpired.

Kula's mother continued her walk up to the box and began calling softly. When she was about fifteen meters from it, little

Kula walked out, looked around, saw his mother and then ran up to her. She quickly smelled his body and accepted him completely. She then walked up to the box and sniffed at it thoroughly. After examining the box, the lioness returned to Kula, and together they walked back to the rest of the pride.

Joy watched as Kula gamboled and played with his two littermates in the headlights of her vehicle. It was a heartwarming scene. Kula's mother's behavior was uncanny. She could not have seen, heard or even scented Kula, yet it was clear that she knew that he was inside the box. And despite the presence of vehicles and humans, she was undeterred and showed great willingness to care. Despite having been separated from Kula for almost three weeks, she acted as a devoted and caring mother.

I witnessed my own lions' willingness to care and share concern for me on many occasions. They viewed me unconditionally as a much-loved member of the pride. On two separate occasions, for example, my lions sensed when I was unwell and dramatically changed their usual movements within their growing territory.

At that time, my pride was ranging over increasingly large distances and only visited me at the camp from time to time in the evenings. However, on both the occasions when I was unwell, the lions ceased roaming in their widening range—and stayed in the local vicinity of the camp. Each day, the lions came to me early in the morning and stayed for a while before moving away to lie up for most of the day. They reappeared in the afternoon and stayed near me until after dusk. As I lay upon my stretcher beside the fence, the lions greeted me lovingly, then lay up around me. Once I was well again, the lions immediately reverted to their normal movement patterns, hunting and exploring their range once again—and visiting me at the camp in the evenings only every few days or so.

Meditation/Visualization Scene
WILLINGNESS TO CARE

1. Go to your peaceful place (remember, if indoors, play a relaxation tape/CD of soothing music).

2. Sit down in a comfortable position, close your eyes and begin to relax. Breathe in slowly, hold your breath for two seconds, then breathe cut. Try to continue to breathe like this throughout the session.

3. As you begin to relax, feel yourself becoming connected with the earth. Beginning with your head, then neck and shoulders, feel yourself drawn downward to the earth.

4. After several minutes, when you feel relaxed and at peace, visualize Tau and Ngala's willingness to care for each other. Become Kula's mother; fill yourself with her devotion. Sense and breathe in my lions' willingness to care when I was unwell. Say to yourself, "Such caring can blossom in my own heart and mind and I will show such caring to others."

5. Do this for several minutes. Feel the power of the precept.

Lion Power! Precept Four
AFFECTION—"LOVE BY ANOTHER NAME"

Affection is love by another name, is it not? The love between George Adamson and his lions and the love between my lions and me is the unconditional kind of love. It is a love that I can only describe as being like a light, reflecting from a beautiful crystal in all directions. It is a light that reflects to and from our souls, a love that I believe transcends what is referred to as "death" and reflects into the spheres beyond. It is an indelible love.

I saw the kind of love of which I write many times between George and his lions in the twilight of the old man's life. One such occasion took place on New Year's Eve 1988. I had noticed that as the new year approached George became increasingly withdrawn. I felt that this was in part because before Joy's death the Adamsons, though living separate lives, would be reunited most Christmases. The new year would also mark the eighth anniversary of Joy's murder.

What also compounded George's low mood at the time was the fact that his wild pride, consisting of Growe, One Eye, Maggie and the others, had not visited the old man at Kampi ya Simba for almost a month. It was clear that he was worried about the pride's whereabouts and badly wanted them to reappear. I knew that if the pride did reappear, it would be the one important thing that would release him from his melancholy.

I have no doubt that the pride, specifically old Growe, could sense George's emotions. One of George's trackers had once described the telepathic communication between the old man and his lions as being "as if the lions and George have [two-way] radios in their hearts and through their hearts can speak to one another."

On New Year's Eve, George and I sat with three young camp visitors around a table that was illuminated by one of the old Tilley lights. We chatted quietly while waiting to see in the new year. Just ten minutes before the chimes of Big Ben would ring out from George's radio, tuned in to faraway London, something magical happened. Suddenly, George and I felt the presence of a lion. I turned and looked into the darkness beyond the camp's fence while George reached for his torch. He shined the torch through the fence and there was old Growe, calm and beautiful. She had come, having heard George's silent inner call for her from miles away.

The old man then rose, fetched some meat and went out into the night to be with her. While she fed, the chimes on the radio rang out and a champagne cork popped. That moment, of Growe coming to the old man's inner call, typified the great affection of a lion, living wild and free, for the old man. That New Year's Eve, George's last, had been blessed by a lion. For a man who lived for lions, it was all he would have wished for.

After George's murder eight months later, his old friend Major Dougie Collins valiantly ran Kampi ya Simba until I arrived at Kora to relocate George's cubs to Botswana. Until the day that Dougie finally left Kampi ya Simba, he made daily entries in George's diary. He also went down regularly to George's grave to water the dozen desert roses that he had planted there after George's funeral. Two days after the funeral, Dougie had witnessed an extraordinary sign of the lions' great love for George, a love that transcends death. He recorded what he witnessed in the diary.

He had gone down to the grave with a bucket of water for the desert roses. The night before, the wind had blown strongly and had scattered the wreaths and flowers which had been placed on George's grave. When Dougie reached the grave, he saw that only one wreath remained upon the cairn of stones. Of this he later stated:

> I noticed lots of spoor and saw where a whole pride had slept near the grave as though on guard. I then noticed a curious thing. The beautiful wreath in particular was now lying on George's grave in an entirely different position. Watching where I placed my feet, so as to not disturb the spoor marks that were clearly imprinted in the soft pink sand, I investigated. I picked up the wreath and clearly saw lion teeth marks on the ribbon and the wreath itself. From the cairn of quartz stones I carefully backtracked the spoor of one large male lion to where it had evidently picked up the windblown wreath to replace it on the grave. There could be no other explanation![63]

Of this extraordinary event, Dougie later commented:

the observations and remarks of mine are not made
by some fanciful romantic, but by a white hunter,
professionally trained over the long years in bush
lore ... in camp that night, alone and in a thoughtful
mood under the same stunted thorn and moon,
I saluted his memory ... for the lions had not
forgotten!

Batian, Furaha and Rafiki had also walked around and onto
George's grave just before I relocated them to the Tuli bushlands.
I have seen video footage of this and in Sandy Gall's book *Lord
of the Lions*[64] there is a picture of Rafiki climbing onto the cairn
of stones on the grave. She held some flowers in her mouth.
The photograph is captioned, "One of the cubs keeps watch
over George's grave the day after the funeral."

I witnessed lion love transcending death two years later when
Batian, at the age of three, was murdered by trophy hunters. As
I mentioned earlier, after his death I built a cairn of stones over
his grave. On the cairn I placed a slab of sandstone upon which
I had engraved the following:

BATIAN
JULY 1988–JULY 1991

After his death I would sit in the afternoons, terribly ag-
grieved, beside the cairn.

One evening before she returned to her cubs, Furaha, Batian's
sister, walked with me down to the grave. There, as I sat on one
side of the cairn, Furaha sat on the other. The sun lowered with
a growing blaze on the western horizon. It was unusually quiet
and Furaha and I strongly sensed Batian's presence around us.
Beyond a stream an impala herd crossed in front of us. They
did not see Furaha and me. We watched them pass, then later
we rose and headed back to the camp in the golden light.

The following evening, I went down to Batian's grave alone. There, at the grave, to my utter surprise, I saw the footprints of lion cubs around the stone cairn. I realized that the night before Rafiki and her small cubs had walked to where Furaha and I had sat the previous afternoon. Both had felt the connection with Batian at that quiet place. I touched the little pug marks and my mood lightened. We were all connected to the same love.

In September 1985 a lioness that I had named Geniessa died in the Tuli bushlands. She was a member of Darky's Lower Majale pride, and five months prior to her death she gave birth to three cubs, a male and two females. It is the life of these cubs, their relationship with other young lions, which further illustrates the affection and caring love that exists among lions.

Early in September, Geniessa was not to be found with the pride, yet her cubs were. Because of this strange situation I searched for her, but without much success. As the days passed, her cubs, once plucky and playful, were becoming increasingly thin and sad-looking.

At that time, and unknown to me, Geniessa was nursing great pain. She had disappeared from the pride because she had stepped into a poacher's rusting snare. It had tightened around her left paw, and as she fought the snare the first digits on her paws were torn off. After releasing herself she limped away in great pain to lie up in a quiet place of dappled light. For many days and nights she remained there, licking at her wounds.

One morning, almost two weeks later, I realized she had moved from the quiet place she had found. On the ground I saw the distinctive dragging tracks as she had moved into open country at the lower part of the Majale River. I followed her tracks and eventually found her. I called the reserve's veterinarian on my two-way radio and informed him of the situation. Later, Geniessa was darted and, to my astonishment, at the impact of the tranquilizing dart, she ran—despite her injury.

When she was unconscious, and her injury had been examined, a decision was made (neither by the vet nor by me, but rather by the reserve's management) that she should be put down. I was immensely angered by this decision. It was undoubtedly one of the saddest incidents to occur during my early studies of lions, and it was a turning point in my life. The survival of Geniessa, a lioness whom I had grown to love, had been imperative to me. I felt that no matter how grisly the wound she should ultimately have been given the chance to survive—but she was not.

As she died that day, her cubs were resting with the Lower Majale pride. The sub-adults of the pride had become particularly affectionate to the little ones. The cubs were still at an age where they needed to suckle. Suckling from the mother lioness is important supplementary feeding for cubs at this age, and the cubs were losing condition. When I next saw the pride, with Geniessa's memory in my mind, it was sad to see the little cubs attempting to suckle at the long-dried-up teats of the adult lionesses and pushing determinedly up to the taut belly of Zonas, a sub-adult lioness.

By the end of 1985 the sub-adults of the pride were spending more and more time away from the adults, and the little cubs moved with them. It was most heartrending to see the sub-adults moving off into the night with these three cubs following behind with hurried little steps.

Despite being fully accepted and adopted by the sub-adults, Geniessa's cubs continued to lose condition. At the beginning of March, a young elephant was found with a smashed leg and was put down. I decided that in order to help the cubs I would drag the elephant's carcass to where I knew they and the sub-adults were lying up. As I unchained the carcass from my Land Rover, all the lions scampered toward it.

The elephant carcass proved to be a godsend for the small cubs. For almost a week the youngsters feasted on it. One evening, ten days later, I found the sub-adults and the cubs as they were setting out to hunt. The difference in the young cubs' condition was dramatic. Their previously almost mangy coats had been transformed into gleaming gold, their faces seemed fuller—and for the first time in many weeks, I saw them playing, a sure indication that their inner beings were beginning to heal.

Several weeks later, the Lower Majale sub-adults had a territorial fight with sub-adults of a neighboring pride. Just prior to the confrontation, I watched in amazement as the sub-adults led the three little ones to some boulders and hid them there for protection. Afterward the sub-adults moved back to where they had hidden the cubs. I followed them to the rocks, and saw them calling softly to the little ones. The cubs emerged and then ran forward to frantically greet and lick their older friends.

In the months ahead, Geniessa's three orphans filled out and matured. I named the smaller male of the trio Little Darky, for I felt and imagined that he looked as Darky would have looked at that age. Little Darky's small but developing mane held promise that it would grow into a thick mass like that of his "father"—and his facial features, even at that stage, were remarkably similar to Darky's.

The young male developed a close and inseparable friendship with Bruno, a sub-adult male who was over a year older, and twice his size. When resting the two young males would always lie together, and when setting off on a hunt with the others they always walked side by side. In time, as a developing young male, Bruno left the pride and Little Darky went with him. Where they went I did not discover, but I wrote at the time:

> Perhaps, one day, they will return once again as
> adults to the Lower Majale, hungry for territory,
> full-bodied and strong. Perhaps they will return
> with grand manes blowing softly in the wind and will
> roar thunderously over the land of their birth....

Meditation/Visualization Scene
AFFECTION

1. Go to your peaceful place (remember, if indoors, play a relaxation tape/CD of soothing music).

2. Sit down in a comfortable position, close your eyes and begin to relax. Breathe in slowly, hold your breath for two seconds, then breathe out. Try to continue to breathe like this throughout the session.

3. As you begin to relax, feel yourself becoming connected with the earth. Beginning with your head, then neck and shoulders, feet yourself drawn downward to the earth.

4. After several minutes, when you feel relaxed and at peace, visualize the love and affection told of in this chapter. Visualize the love between George and Growe that New Year's Eve and the connection that I felt with Furaha at Batian's grave. Think about and visualize the affection shown by the sub-adults to Geniessa's little ones. Infuse yourself with such love and affection. Let this love open within you like the petals of a beautiful and eternal rose. Let this love be a forever thing within you.

5. Do this for several minutes. Feel the power of the precept.

CHAPTER 6

Lion Power!
The Seven Vital
Precepts of the Lion

Part II:

Living Your Life with Lion Power!

Lion Power! Precept Five
THE DETERMINATION OF THE DAUGHTERS

Determined, vital, purposeful, tenacious, resolute. All these words describe the spirits of the two lionesses Furaha and Rafiki. Furaha was particularly confident in all that she did. Rafiki, while equally as determined as her sister, was a little more wary in her ways. The following story describes, in a humorous sense, aspects of their determined natures.

One afternoon the lions and I were resting in the shade of a large tree close to a waterhole that the summer rains had recently replenished. As I was busy writing notes, I saw Furaha suddenly rouse in a flurry and stand looking very alert in the direction of the waterhole. Her sudden movements quickly alerted Batian and Rafiki, awaking them from their slumbers with a start. I turned to look toward the waterhole and saw, to my utter surprise, a bull elephant less than fourteen meters away from us.

Instantly, I felt tiny as I looked up at the elephant. Elephants, despite their bulk, are well known to move silently through the bush—hence they are known by some bush dwellers as "gray ghosts." I had not heard a whisper of the bull's approach.

My reaction to the sight was almost instantaneous. I fled. My papers dropped from my hands, were caught by a sudden gust of wind and flew into the air like giant confetti. As I reached the bank of a small streambed, I turned to look back. Batian, I quickly noticed, had also fled and was standing next to me. The lionesses, though, made of stronger stuff than us males, had remained by the tree.

To my astonishment (and to much concern), I saw Furaha begin to move into a stalking position. Rafiki too began to crouch down. Both lionesses slowly crept forward and, hiding behind logs and bushes, advanced toward the elephant. At this point, though, the bull was very much aware of our presence and was twisting his trunk in the air in an attempt to catch our scent.

To my consternation, I saw the two sisters creep even closer. At that point I had visions of the two lionesses being slammed against the trees by powerful sweeps of the bull's trunk. Then the unexpected happened. The bull let out a loud, high-pitched trumpet, swung around and crashed away into the bush. His hindquarters, as he ran, were reminiscent of someone wearing baggy, wrinkled old trousers, ten sizes too big.

The two determined lionesses bounded after the elephant. It was only at that point that Batian and I came out of the shadows. I watched with amusement as Batian, now keen to join the game, hurriedly attempted to catch up with his sisters.

I stood alone and listened as the sounds of the elephant charging through the bush became increasingly distant. While I waited for my lions to return, I walked around to search for all my scattered notes. Some twenty minutes later, three happy, panting lions reappeared. They drank thirstily from the waterhole and greeted me enthusiastically. It was very apparent that they had thoroughly enjoyed seeing off the elephant. Before we returned to camp, the lions rested beneath the tree while I fruitlessly searched for one last missing page of my notes—which, incidentally, I never found.

As Rafiki and Furaha entered into young adulthood, I witnessed a more serious form of determination, a determination that combined loyalty and deep love, toward me. The following story demonstrates this determination.

One evening, my small pride appeared at my camp after having been away in the eastern portion of their territory for several days. As usual, they greeted me affectionately, and during our fond greeting I suddenly noticed that a large fluid-filled membrane hung from Rafiki's vulva. I became concerned, as I feared that she was in the early stages of miscarrying cubs. At that time, I had not, because of her young age, even suspected that she could have been pregnant.

Rafiki, apart from occasionally licking the membrane, otherwise seemed perfectly fine within herself and later happily bounded away with her brother and sister into the twilight. The following morning, I, the concerned "parent," set out to search for her. Despite tracking her for several hours, I was unsuccessful. That afternoon, I returned to the search and quite suddenly came across Rafiki alone, not far from camp. It was as if she simply materialized in front of me. Immediately, I noticed that there was no sign of the membrane, or of any bleeding.

Strangely, though, she did not wish to return to the camp with me. Instead, in her own special way of calling and skipping, she clearly indicated that she wanted me to follow her. Puzzled, I did follow her for a while, but as the sun began to set I had to stop and turn back toward the camp. There I found Batian, and fifteen minutes later Rafiki reappeared. She indicated again that she wished us to follow her.

That night she and Batian stayed close to the camp, and in my tent, before falling asleep, I pondered why she was so determined to indicate that she wanted us to follow her. What was it that she wanted us to see or go to?

Early the following morning I saw Rafiki beside the camp's fence. Once again, she repeated the behavior of the previous day. I stepped out of the camp and with Batian beside me began following her through the bush. We followed her for over an hour and during that time she repeatedly turned around, called to us, then continued to lead the way. She led us up onto a rise, then entered a particularly thick clump of bush beside a small crevice. I saw her climb down into a thicket and then, while hidden, heard her calling us. Batian stepped forward and ventured to where she was. I watched as he peered downward into the thicket. He remained there, unmoving, for several minutes, then moved backward and lay down.

As he moved aside, I stepped forward. I looked into the thicket and saw Rafiki nestled in the bushes with a perfectly formed, though dead, cub lying between her paws. I was amazed. She had been so determined to lead us to see the cub. I felt a strange mixture of emotions: greatly sad for Rafiki that the cub had been stillborn, and at the same time touched and enormously privileged that she had so wanted Batian and me to see the little one.

In the months ahead, both Rafiki and Furaha successfully gave birth to litters of cubs and both lionesses blessed me by deliberately and determinedly leading me to their newborns. I would sit just meters away as they nursed their cubs. This extract from my daily diary marks the special day Rafiki led me to her litter of four cubs.

> It is an incredible privilege to sit upon a riverbank, watching a lioness with tiny cubs without fear, just pride. It is an incredible feeling when Rafiki leaves her cubs to greet me. It's a magical merging of our lives.

Both Rafiki and Furaha proved to be determined and devoted mothers. This was demonstrated to me many times, but one particular occasion will always stay in my mind. One day I found where they had attempted to dig a warthog family out of their burrow. They had been unsuccessful, but in bizarre circumstances the entire warthog family (consisting of a male, a female and a litter of piglets) had suffocated, trapped in the burrow.

It was an incredibly hot period, drought was pervading the area and at times the responsibility of providing meat for the ever-growing cubs in such conditions sapped the lionesses' energy. With this in mind, I decided that I would load the dead piglets into my jeep and give them to the lionesses should they appear at my camp in the next day or so.

In the late afternoon, the pride did indeed appear at the camp. After the lionesses and I greeted each other, I gave them each a piglet. I expected them to begin eating immediately, as it was obvious that they had not fed recently. Instead, I witnessed the unexpected. Neither lioness fed, but instead walked, piglet in mouth, to their cubs and presented the food to them. They then returned to me and I gave them both a second piglet. They repeated their action until I had handed them the last piglets. Then, as the cubs fed noisily, I sat with their mothers, watching the little ones in the twilight. My lion daughters had shown such determined selflessness. It was very moving.

As I mentioned earlier, Furaha and the cubs Sala and Tana were tried, convicted, then sentenced to death for a crime they did not commit. With Batian killed by trophy hunters a year earlier, this tragedy left Rafiki and me as the last of the pride. Tough as it was, she and I walked through our sorrow. One absolute certainty is that life carries on, and Nelion, a beautiful male lion, came into Rafiki's life. In turn, she had a litter of cubs (which, once again, she led me to). For many complicated reasons, it was just afterward that I decided (partly to protect Rafiki) to leave the Tuli bushlands. One of the last times that I saw Rafiki, she was walking in golden light on the wide open plain below my camp. She was returning to her cubs after having visited me. The very last time that Rafiki and I were together, we were sitting on a hillside that was basked in a very deep orange, almost red light. Then, as the last light was about to give way to the night, she rose and rubbed her head against me. I stroked her head, knowing that this could be our final farewell. She then moved away, called to her cubs who were lying up nearby, then with her family disappeared from sight.

Rafiki is, as I write, twelve years old. She is a grandmother, and she roams her territory in the Tuli bushlands with her pride, her family of eight. Through all the hardship, the tragedies and the despair we shared, Rafiki and her pride represent to me triumph over adversity. Through her and her offspring and their offspring, other lions will continue to be born free—and so the Adamson lions live on.

Whenever I feel a little sadness thinking of Batian, Furaha, Sala and Tana, I visualize Rafiki and her pride living wild and free. I visualize the cubs that have been born since I last saw Rafiki and the wonderful cubs that are still to be born in my lions' secret places in the future. I know that without great determination, my own and the lions', this miracle would not have been possible. When I tell myself this, I feel blessed and immensely privileged. Though now physically apart from her, I speak to the determined Rafiki in my mind, and from time to time she, Furaha and Batian visit me in my dreams.

Mysteriously, Furaha manifested herself, long after her death, to a very good friend of mine. It is a strange but wonderful story. Kate Turkington is a living legend in the broadcasting world in southern Africa. She is an author, a former academic, radio and television talk-show host, travel writer and journalist. In her earlier days with the BBC, she interviewed everyone from the Prime Minister to the Beatles and even a talking dog! At one stage, she covered royal events and in turn met most of the royals.

Kate and I first met when I was working as a game ranger in the Tuli bushlands over seventeen years ago. She sees me as her "adopted" son.

Kate hosts one of South Africa's longest running talk-radio programs, *Believe It, or Not*, which deals with matters of faith, religion, ethics and morals. Three years ago, while on a spiritual expedition in South America, she "saw," encountered and greeted Furaha. One night, on the banks of the Amazon River, the expedition leader encouraged Kate and the other "pilgrims" to connect with their power animal. "Empty your mind of everything," they were told. Kate closed her eyes and pushed away fragments of cynicism. The following (from Kate's book *There's More to Life than Surface*)[65] is an account in her own words of what took place.

> Suddenly, I am standing ankle-deep in a sunlit forest pool. There is total silence. Before me is a thin high waterfall. I wade across its fine falling spray and push my way through the curtain of water. I am now in another pool, similar to the first, also surrounded by trees and plants, equally still and quiet. A shallow, sloping white sandy beach is at the far side of the pool. I wade over to the white beach and take a few steps up it. The silence seems to intensify. The stillness is almost tangible.
>
> Then—there is a movement in the bushes. I turn my head toward the sound. The leaves part and, as I watch, a lioness comes toward me, golden and glowing in the sunshine. She comes up to me and looks at me with great golden-green eyes. We both stand still. Then as if by some pre-arranged sign, some remembered behavior on my part, I put my arms around her and lay my face along her flanks. She is soft and warm. A feeling of utter peace and joy comes over me. I do not want the moment to end. We hold this position for a moment or two, and then she gently moves away. She pads down to the pool, crouches and laps the clear, bright water. When she has finished drinking, she gets up and walks back the way she has come toward the undergrowth. As she goes

past me, she pauses and wraps her long tall around me, almost like an embrace. Then she vanishes into the bushes as silently as she has come.

The silence is absolute.

I stand for a moment, then wade back through the waterfall, the way I came.

I open my eyes and find myself on the banks of the Amazon.

Several weeks later, Kate and I met up and she told me this remarkable story. I asked her to describe the lioness to me, and from her description I sensed strongly who the lioness was. Almost as a confirmation of what I was thinking, I asked Kate what the last thing was that the lioness did before she left her.

"The lioness curled her tall around me like a loving embrace," she replied.

Kate was describing a greeting characteristic that my lions would always do to me. They would use their tails to almost embrace me.

I said to Kate, "That was Furaha."

My lion daughters had such love and such determination. They are inspirations and emblazon the need to tap into the vital force of living with vigor, of the zest of living in every moment; to feel the vitality in everything, to feel and to love life with vitality.

Furaha is physically dead, but yet through her spirit brought such peace, love and inspiration to Kate. Furaha's determined vitality lives on.

Meditation/Visualization Scene
DETERMINATION

1. Go to your peaceful place (remember, play a relaxation tape/CD of soothing music).

2. Sit down in a comfortable position, close your eyes and begin to relax. Breathe in slowly, hold your breath for two

seconds, then breathe out. Try to continue to breathe like this throughout the session.

3. As you begin to relax, feel yourself becoming connected with the earth. Beginning with your head, then neck and shoulders, feel yourself drawn downward to the earth.

4. After several minutes, when you feel relaxed and at peace, visualize the determination, the vitality, of Furaha and Rafiki. Visualize Rafiki's determination in wanting me to follow her to see the cubs. Feel her determination in her wanting me to sit close by as she nursed her cubs. Tap into Rafiki's and Furaha's selfless determination to put their cubs before themselves. Draw on the vitality of the spirit of the beautiful Furaha.

5. Do this for several minutes. Feel the power of the precept.

Lion Power! Precept Six
THE COURAGE OF A SON

Batian was born with a very courageous heart, but as a small cub this led him at times into misadventure. Once, for example, he decided to walk up to one of George Adamson's wild lionesses, who was standing on the other side of the fence at Kampi ya Simba. The wild lioness suddenly noticed Batian standing beside her. She snarled, and for being overbold and underrespectful of an adult, Batian was sent tumbling against the fence by a swat from the lioness's paw.

On another occasion, it was a bird that sent him scampering away after being too bold. With us at Kampi ya Simba lived a cackling mob of vulturine guinea fowl that George would feed daily. Throughout the day, members of this flock could be found in various parts of the camp, and not uncommonly several could be found in the cubs' enclosure. The guinea fowl were a source of fascination to the cubs when they were still small. They were at times almost mesmerized by their cackling and bustle.

Later the cubs would try to stalk the birds, but whenever they got close they would inevitably lose their nerve and scamper, heads low, back to the sanctuary of their wooden "cub-house"— a wooden structure in which they would sleep at night.

One day, though, Batian seemed intent on pouncing on and seizing one particular guinea fowl. He fixed his eyes intently on the bird and, with as much seriousness as a cub can muster, began stalking toward it. The guinea fowl, with its back to Batian, was oblivious to the cub's measured approach.

Closer and closer Batian stalked, until he was just fifteen centimeters from where the bird was busily pecking and scraping at the ground. As Batian was positioning himself into a pre-leaping position, the unexpected happened. The guinea fowl, intent on scraping and pecking, suddenly leaped backward, bumping into Batian's face. The cub let out a squawk of alarm, leaped into the air, then scampered as fast as his little paws could take him to the safety of the cub-house. The guinea fowl, after pausing briefly to look disdainfully in the direction that Batian had run, continued its pecking and scraping.

A year-and-a-half later, now in the Tuli bushlands, my lions, particularly Batian, were having more serious confrontations than those with the guinea fowl at Kora. The rehabilitation project was going well, and at the age of twenty months the lions were killing more often for themselves and were slowly establishing territory. Despite the fact that the project was going well, I would on occasion keep the lions inside their enclosure if I knew other lions were in the vicinity. On reflection, I realize that I was being over-cautious and had underestimated my lions' sense of belonging.

One day I found the fresh tracks of four young lions not far from the camp. That night, I led my lions into the enclosure for protection. Very early the following morning, the four lions came to the camp, and I awoke to hear, then see, Batian attempting to attack the intruders from within the enclosure. He was furious that the four strangers were standing just meters from him and was frustrated that he could not chase them away. After that night, I never again kept my pride within the enclosure. From then on, they were completely free.

At sunrise, I opened the enclosure gate and the lions tumbled out quickly to investigate where the four strangers had been. My lions, I reflected, were no longer large cubs but young sub-adults with a great sense of belonging in their wild home and were fueled with determination to defend this territory.

Batian quickly headed to "his" scent-marking trees. To his indignation, they had been jetted upon by the strangers the night before. Quickly but thoroughly, he righted this wrong and marked his trees, doing so repeatedly that evening and again the following morning.

A month or so later, a direct confrontation took place between my lions and the four sub-adults. I not only witnessed confrontation, but also became embroiled in it as a member of my small pride. This happened one morning as I was following the tracks where my three had walked the night before.

Suddenly I heard the sounds of loud growls and snarls about a kilometer away. Concerned, I began running in the direction of the sounds. After climbing up a hillside I came out onto the edge of an open plain. I saw three lions moving toward where I discovered Batian engaged in a fierce conflict with a male who was a little older than him. Then I saw Rafiki and Furaha heading toward these lions.

It was at this moment that I was filled by the sense of being an integral part of my pride. The need to be involved in this territorial confrontation, to protect our territory, surged through me. On this occasion it was as if I transformed almost physically into a lion, I empathized so deeply with what was occurring in my lions' lives.

I called to my lions, not as a human, but in the "Oooweh," lion way that I had learned from them—the way that they would call to each other and to me. Rafiki and Furaha heard my call, turned and looked in my direction. Batian then appeared from the fray in the thick bush. My pride then ran up to me, greeted me and, after regrouping, turned to launch in the direction of the watching sub-adults. I ran with them; the sub-adults turned to flee and we then chased them for more than a kilometer-and-a-half. With the four strangers gone, my lions greeted me with exceptional affection and then, visibly very excited, began to scent-mark thoroughly on trees and bushes. They were doing this to emphasize their victory and that the land was theirs. They belonged.

That night and the following day my pride remained in the area where the confrontation had taken place and this further denoted a strong statement of territorial ownership. I held great pride in my heart at that time. George's last lion orphans were now truly wild and free, and—most importantly—they belonged.

In the months that followed, Batian blossomed into a fine, large young male. I estimated that when fully grown he would be one of the largest male lions to have lived in the Tuli bushlands.

At times, he had confrontations with other males but he always fought them head-on, and in time the confrontations became less common. Batian also reached the point of maturing in that he began seeking out a mate. This new stage of his life occurred one special evening in the winter of 1991. We, Batian and I, were sitting together north of the camp on a plain. As the sun began to set, I stood up, stroked Batian and began to walk back toward the camp. To my surprise, he did not follow me, but stood up and began heading off in a northwesterly direction. I will always remember the sight of him on the plain, silhouetted by the beautiful sky, now entering a new phase of his life. He disappeared for several days. I tracked him the following day and discovered where he had found and joined up with a young lioness. After seeing their tracks together, I turned around and headed back to camp. I was delighted that he had found a mate,

After this Batian would regularly head off to the northwest to be with his lioness. She in turn gave birth to cubs. Today, somewhere in the Tuli bushlands, there are descendants from that litter of cubs produced by the union of Batian and the young lioness.

Batian, the courageous, was killed by white trophy hunters on a South African game farm. Two months earlier he was attacked by two nomadic males. My lions were feeding on a kill when these lions suddenly confronted them. A short but very savage battle ensued between the males and Batian. Batian fought with incredible courage, and the fact that afterward I found him alive was testament to this. But against two males of his own size, it was tragically inevitable that he would be dealt devastating injuries.

From the camp I heard the sounds of the confrontation. I ran in their direction, and as I reached a streambed two golden forms dashed toward me—Furaha and Rafiki. After greeting me they led me to Batian. He was in a terrible state: his tail had been bitten off completely and he was in deep shock. I crouched in front of him and brushed aside his mane hair. There I saw deep wounds on his neck. Long canines had been buried deeply into the nape and had torn and exposed the muscles. His body was crisscrossed with long, bloody cuts, raking wounds inflicted by the claws of his attackers.

I could not tranquilize Batian and move him to the safety of the cubs' enclosure at camp because the combination of the shock and the drugs would have killed him. Instead I made him as comfortable as possible, encouraged him to drink and administered large doses of antibiotics given to me by a vet friend who by good fortune was visiting the bushlands at the time. Additionally, I sprayed antibiotic powder into his wounds and onto his stump of a tail.

I stayed with Batian in the bush for three days and nights, treating his wounds, encouraging him to drink—at times even resorting to trickling rehydration fluids into his mouth. It was an enormously tense time.

After the third night, when his condition seemed to have stabilized and when he seemed much more aware of everything around him, I tranquilized him, moved him onto the back of my truck and took him to camp. There, on a drip, as three liters of glucose trickled into him, he was operated on by my vet friend, then we carried him into the cubs' enclosure to recover. After the operation I felt optimistic. Today, I feel that what I was drawing on and sensing then was Batian's own courageous spirit and his will to survive.

Early the following morning, I entered the enclosure to check on him. As I did so, to my amazement this brave, battle-torn lion stood up. Then, despite his tottering legs, he determinedly moved forward and greeted me. He staggered over to where he knew the water bowl was. He drank and drank. Later he even ate some meat.

Over the next few days he ate well and his condition remained stable. He then went into a dramatic stage of self-healing, often lying in the sun on his back, which helped drain a tremendous amount of fluid from his neck injuries. "Remarkable" does not begin to adequately describe his recovery. By the second week after the fight and the operation, his dreadful wounds were healing visibly, he had gained much weight and his muscles were again becoming taut. By the third week, he was beginning to spend days away from the camp.

At the time, certain pessimists thought that he would never again lead the life of a wild lion, that the loss of his tail would severely affect his balance. Instead, he adapted and in time could run as strongly as he ever could before the fight. He had healed in an extraordinary way and I was constantly amazed by his courageous spirit, which had remained unbroken despite the near-death ordeal. After the fight and the trauma he could have become a nervous and territorially insecure lion. Instead, as he healed he began to advertise his presence in the bushlands by calling territorially. He began, once again, to roar at the dawn.

Through his recovery and his indomitable spirit, Batian was teaching me about true courage, a courage that I can continue to draw upon to this day—Batian's courage. I draw upon this courage whenever I stand up in front of an audience to present my lecture on my life with lions. I draw on it whenever I face adversity, including when I have received death threats in recent years after exposing cases of vicious cruelty to wild animals. And as I was preparing to write this portion of this book, I drew on Batian's courage for a three-week-old cub that was unwell.

A vet called me just a few days ago to ask for my advice on this cub. It was one of a litter of four. Two had already died. The cub was going downhill and would not suckle. I gave the vet advice concerning milk formulas and so on but, equally important, I later visualized the cub and projected Batian's courage onto him. Yesterday, the vet called me again. She was very happy. The cub, she told me, was now doing very well, was suckling hungrily and seemed to be well on the way to recovery. It is my belief that Batian's courage, in part, enabled this recovery to take place.

Meditation/Visualization Scene
COURAGE

1. Go to your peaceful place (remember, if indoors, play a relaxation tape/CD of soothing music).

2. Sit down in a comfortable position, close your eyes and begin to relax. Breathe in slowly, hold your breath for two seconds, then breathe out. Try to continue to breathe like this throughout the session.

3. As you begin to relax, feel yourself becoming connected with the earth. Beginning with your head, then neck and shoulders, feel yourself drawn downward to the earth.

4. After several minutes, when you feel relaxed and at peace, feel Batian's remarkable courage; the courage with which he lived his life; the amazing courage upon which he drew to make his extraordinary recovery from such severe injuries. Feel such courage within yourself and use it to overcome whatever adversity you may experience in your life. Have the courage of a lion. Let go of fears and courageously go forward, overcome adversity and achieve whatever you want to achieve. Have the courage of a lion—Batian's courage.

5. Do this for several minutes. Feel the power of the precept. Feel the lion's power. Lion Power!

Lion Power! Precept Seven
LOYALTY

In 1977, George Adamson witnessed an extraordinary example of loyalty and love in lions. At that time he was rehabilitating two young lions back into the wilds at Kora. They were brother and sister and George had named them Suleiman and Sheba. Their rehabilitation was progressing well and they were living in the vicinity of a dry sand "lugga" (streambed) some nine kilometers from George's camp. Every few days, George would drive out to the lugga to check on the youngsters.

One day, though, as he was searching for the lions in that area, Sheba suddenly burst out from the riverine bush and ran up to him. George saw that she had scratches on her body and that she was clearly traumatized.

Sheba turned to look in the direction from which she had come, then began heading back. George followed her and Sheba led him through the bush for several hundred meters. Something was clearly wrong and the old man became increasingly worried about Suleiman.

As Sheba and George approached a gap in the dense bush, he saw that the ground was crisscrossed and scarred by a myriad of lion, hippopotamus and crocodile tracks. Then he saw Suleiman. He lay dead beneath a large acacia tree with terrible wounds to his chest and stomach.

Shocked by the sight, George began to scan the ground to try to understand what had taken place. Gradually he was able to piece the tragedy together.

It seemed that Suleiman and Sheba had surprised a large hippo bull that had been on its way back to the river after a night of grazing inland. Almost suicidally, considering the enormous size of the hippo, the brother and sister had attacked it. Then an incredible battle took place with the hippo finally forcing Suleiman against a clump of trees and fatally wounding him with a massive bite of its jaws.

George learned from the signs on the ground that Sheba's loyalty to her dead brother had been extraordinary. For three days she had courageously protected her brother's body and had stood guard next to him. Crocodiles had slipped out of the Tana River to attempt to claim the body, but, time and time again, she had circled them and successfully driven them back to the water. Each time she had returned to her brother's side.

George then prepared to bury Suleiman on the riverbank, just above the flood mark. As he was doing this, Sheba sat quietly close by. At dusk, with Suleiman's body buried, George was about to return to his camp. He called to Sheba but she refused to leave the area and remained sitting next to her brother's grave. Such was the great loyalty of Sheba, the lioness.

On a bright, hot day, deep in the Tuli bushlands, Furaha demonstrated a loyalty to me that resulted in her saving my life, or at the very least, saving me from very serious injury. This is what happened.

While out walking with my lions, I came across the fresh tracks of a large male leopard. Batian approached me, then nosed at the area where the leopard's tracks lay imprinted upon the dusty soil. I watched with interest a little later as all three lions walked purposely in the direction in which the tracks led. Lions and leopards are natural competitors. Leopards will, if the opportunity arises, kill and eat lion cubs, and lions will chase, and at times kill, leopards. Therefore I was curious to see that my young lions were deliberately seeking out a leopard that day.

I followed my lions, and just as I stepped up onto a stream bank I heard tremendous snarling and growling. As I looked up, I saw Batian and Furaha pulling themselves up into a small tree. Then I saw a leopard leap out of the tree and race away. The lions pursued him and a great battle broke out between the young lions and the leopard.

After some twenty minutes, the leopard leaped out of another tree toward a dry streambed. The lions followed immediately. By the time I reached the streambed, the leopard, surrounded by lions, had backed himself into a low bush. The fight continued and later I saw the leopard lying on his back in his last defense position, flailing with paws and his jaws at the lions. Later, after some thirty minutes of conflict, I thought that the leopard had been mortally injured. He moved a little and gradually, one by one, the lions drifted away to rest in some nearby shade.

I then joined the panting and bloodied lions in the shady area. Just as I sat down, I noticed the leopard turn over, rise to its feet and, with its head low, begin to move away gingerly. The lions also quickly noticed the movement and this prompted them to rush at the leopard again.

As the fight continued, Batian was caught by two tearing swipes of the leopard's paws on his nose and close to his eyes. Stinging with pain, he retaliated with great force and crashed his paws onto the leopard's head. After this he moved away. The lionesses continued the fight, with Furaha too being caught by the leopard's slashing claws. The leopard split the soft black skin around her mouth and I saw blood dripping on her chin and white chest. She left the leopard to Rafiki and moved away to rest.

Concerned by her injuries, I quietly called to her from the place where I was hidden on the bank of the streambed behind some bushes. Furaha heard my call, turned and headed toward me. Upon reaching me, she sat beside me, facing forward to where the leopard lay in the streambed.

I pulled a water bottle from the bag that I had been carrying and poured water into my hand. While I spoke quietly to her Furaha allowed me to clean her wounds, to stroke her and to inspect the gashes and tears on her mouth. After this she drank some water from my cupped hand.

Then, as I was leaning forward in a semi-crouched position to put the water bottle back into the bag, the leopard (some thirty meters away) saw me for the first time.

Suddenly, without any warning, the leopard spun onto his feet and charged at an extraordinary speed toward me. In one movement I rose and rammed a bullet into the breech of my rifle. During that time, the leopard had already torn up onto the bank and was less than three meters away. Suddenly a shadow of gold crossed in front of me. Furaha launched herself forward and crashed into the leopard. I leapt back, abandoning my bag but keeping the rifle at the ready. Then I saw Batian and Rafiki bounding toward where Furaha and the leopard were fighting.

Later, from a distance, I saw the leopard lying on his back again, surrounded by my lions. At that point I walked back to my camp. Consciously, I wanted to collect my camera; unconsciously, though, I wanted to calm myself and let what had just happened sink in. And indeed what could have happened.

Leopards have been described as perfect killing machines, and when wounded the leopard is one of the most dangerous animals in the world. According to accounts that I have read, a wounded leopard will sink its teeth into a person's shoulder or head and, using its powerful hind legs and lethal claws, rip into the stomach and lower body. Apparently, there are reports of a single wounded leopard mauling five armed human beings in one charge before dashing away. Quite simply, in all likelihood, if it had not been for Furaha's loyalty and extreme bravery I would have been killed or horribly mutilated. My lion daughter had saved me and for this I am eternally grateful to her and her spirit.

Later that day I returned to the vicinity of the fight. I stopped a hundred meters away looking and listening for signs of the lions. I heard nothing other than birds singing and the breeze upon my face. Was the leopard dead or alive? Were my lions still nearby? I decided to call Batian, knowing that if he was with me I would be reasonably safe to venture into the streambed.

Batian then emerged from a clump of mopane trees, followed by Rafiki. Both greeted me very affectionately. I think that they sensed my feelings about venturing into the streambed. As I stepped forward Batian walked alongside me, then as we reached the streambed he led the way, heading toward a thick bush. When we reached the bush I noticed that he began to paw beneath it. I saw the leopard. He lay there with staring, wide eyes, but eyes that saw no more. He was dead. I leaned down to pull his body from beneath the bush into the open. Incredibly, Batian joined me in this task, hooking his claws into the fur and walking and tugging backward.

The leopard had been in his prime. He was over two meters long and weighed, I estimated, at least sixty kilograms. On inspecting his body, I saw that he had been killed by a deep bite (most likely inflicted by Batian) through the nape of his neck.

As the sun set my loyal lions and I moved away, leaving the leopard where he lay. Slowly, we headed back to camp. All four of us were exhausted by the day's dramatic events. I think that a part of me was in shock.

As usual, the following morning I went out into the bush with the lions, and later, when they rested, I returned to the place of the fight. The ground was littered by tracks of hyenas and jackals. The leopard's body had been almost completely consumed by the scavengers. Only some dried blood on stones and tufts of fur caught on dry branches indicated what had happened just a day before. I stood where I had been when the leopard had rushed to attack me, where Furaha had saved me, and I reflected on the entire encounter. What would have happened if she had not been beside me?

Today, when I ponder the incident, its essence reminds me of the enormous loyalty told of in the legend of Androcles and the lion. An ancient Latin version of this tale was recorded in *Attic Nights* by Aulus Gellius in the second century. Gellius quotes a "learned man," Apion, on what he had seen at Rome concerning the man and the lion. Apion's account is as follows:

> In the Great Circus, a battle with wild beasts on a grand scale was being exhibited to the people. Of that spectacle, since I chanced to be in Rome, I was an eyewitness. There were many savage wild beasts, brutes, remarkable for their huge size, and one of these in particular (a lion) surpassed all the rest because of the huge size of his body ... There was brought in ... the slave of an ex-consul; the slave's name was Androcles. When that lion saw him from a distance he stopped short as if in amazement, and then approached the man slowly and quietly, as if he recognized him. Then ... he came close to the man ... and gently licked his feet and hands ... Then you might have seen man and lion exchange joyful greetings, as if they recognized each other.

What then occurred is told in *When Elephants Weep*.[66]

The Emperor Gaius Caesar, known more popularly as Caligula, wanted to know why the lion had spared the man. Androcles related how he had run away from his master into the lonely desert and had hidden in a remote cave. A lion came into the cave with a bleeding paw, groaning and moaning in pain. The lion, Androcles is reported to have said, "approached me mildly and gently, and lifting up his foot, was evidently showing it to me and holding it out as if to ask for help."

Androcles then removed a great splinter from the paw and cared for the injury, whereupon "relieved by that attention and treatment of mine, the lion, putting his paw in my hand, lay down and went to sleep." The man and the lion lived together for three years, living in the cave and the lion hunting for them. Androcles was later recaptured, returned to Rome and sentenced to death in the arena. The Emperor, upon hearing this story, granted freedom to both Androcles and the lion, whereupon they walked the streets together ... and everyone who met them anywhere exclaimed: "This is the lion that was a man's friend, this is the man who was physician to a lion."

It is, quite simply, a beautiful ancient story of friendship and loyalty between a man and a lion. I am blessed to have had my life enriched by such friendship and loyalty.

Meditation/Visualization Scene
LOYALTY

1. Go to your peaceful place (remember, if indoors, play a relaxation tape/CD of soothing music).

2. Sit down in a comfortable position, close your eyes and begin to relax. Breathe in slowly, hold your breath for two seconds, then breathe out. Try to continue to breathe like this throughout the session.

3. As you begin to relax, feel yourself becoming connected with the earth. Beginning with your head, then neck and shoulders, feel yourself drawn downward to the earth.

4. After several minutes, when you feel relaxed and at peace, visualize the loyal Sheba, remaining beside her brother's body and later staying by his grave. Imagine the loyalty of Furaha when she saved me from the attacking leopard. Fill yourself with such loyalty. Make such loyalty a part of your very being. Show great loyalty to those you love and in turn such loyalty will be shown to you—the loyalty of Sheba's and Furaha's great hearts.

5. Do this for several minutes. Feel the power of the precept.

CHAPTER 7

The Pyramid of Life, the Inner Voice & the Reawakening ...

... ask now the beasts, and they shall teach thee ...
Or speak to the earth, and it shall teach thee....

JOB 12: 7-8

*H*ow we lead our lives is ultimately up to us. Those three words, "up to us," can be the key, yet at the same time can also be a contradiction. How we lead our lives is "up to us," but we must ignore the conditioning that society throws at us. "Bigger," "faster," "better," "more," "upgrade," "richer"—these words and more like them have become the new gods since the latter part of the last century. We are even conditioned in how we perceive beauty. A tiny proportion of the world's population are supermodels, yet the media, in all forms, convince us that theirs is the beauty that all women should try to attain.

In the modern age blinders have been placed over our eyes so that we cannot see the big picture. We see only a narrow view of life. Blindered, we can no longer understand the humility of our smallness in relation to a sunset, an ever-flowing waterfall, the changing of the seasons or the majesty of snowcapped mountains. We have lost touch with the earth and the understanding, the reality, that man is just a part of life on earth. We have lost touch with our place in the pyramid of life—so much so that not only do we view ourselves as being at the pinnacle of the pyramid but probably, subconsciously, that we created the pyramid ourselves! We have lost touch with the fact that the pyramid of life, the soil, the trees, the air we breathe, water, the animals, rain and sunlight and ourselves are all part of one community.

Fortunately, a visible shift in perceptions is occurring today. We are letting go of being told what to believe and what not to believe. Today, we are increasingly empowering ourselves as individuals and within the community. We are also at last moving forward, evolving morally, extending rights and considerations to areas beyond our direct self-interest, in issues involving children, women, non-European races and animals.

We are increasingly focusing on developing a healthier mind, body and spirit, and from this empowerment our focus will extend to the health of those around us, the environment—everything around us.

Fundamentally, people do not truly want to harm themselves or others. We all know what is right and what is wrong. This is a part of us. We know that:

- It is wrong to harm.
- It is wrong to create suffering.
- It is wrong to take that which belongs to another.
- It is wrong to kill something or to cause something to be killed.

We know that a smile is better than a grimace, we know that caring is good and that selfishness is not. Within us, it feels right to be kind and it feels wrong to hold anger or malice. We simply know these things. Our being, our inner self, our inner voice tells us these things. All we have to do is to listen to that inner voice.

At times we are tempted to do something for our own selfish gain and at the risk of hurting someone or something. At times we are tempted to lie or to betray someone. We might do such things, but not before the inner voice tells us not to, that it is wrong. We need to listen to that inner voice much more. It is our ethical voice.

Just imagine the world we could live in if we made ethical considerations globally before acting. The rainforests would not be felled, the seas would not be polluted, we would not inflict the earth with the calamities that we have created through our actions. By bringing in and acting upon our ethical considerations, by listening to our inner voice, we would have a calmer, quieter and ecologically more sound world around us.

I do believe that the inner voice, sometimes just a whisper, sometimes a loud clarion call, is starting to be heard. Many of us today are at last beginning to see once more that the inhabitants of the natural world are our fellow constituents of the only home we all share.

Perceptions about the "beasts" are changing rapidly. The lion is, for example, tremendously better loved today than it was in the recent past—and so too is the wolf. These major changes in attitude have occurred in a few short decades, and I believe, despite what we feel sometimes, that we are evolving morally.

We will continue to head toward increasing spiritual re-awakening as long as we realize that the connection between ourselves and the natural world is essential to our health and that of the planet. We will go forward spiritually by reopening ourselves to learning from special beings such as the lion—as realized by our ancestors through the ages.

We cannot lose the lion or the other animals of great inspiration, or any more species on earth. They should be nurtured and protected for their own sake. We have much to learn from the animals and their wild domains. Our own destiny on earth is, I believe, reliant on the existence of these ancient and long ago perfected forms of life. Their existence creates in man a memory of his own roots in nature, roots that if severed spiritually and forgotten would inevitably result in the spiritual demise of mankind. We must remember the words of Credo Mutwa: "without the lion and other cats, a great spiritual darkness would descend upon all life." These great beings remind us that we and all life are born of one mother, the earth, and without them and the wild places we would suffer from dire loneliness of heart. We would become a lonely nation of life.

And this is why the seven principles of the lion are so important. The principles enable us to draw from the lion and nature essences that can fuel us so that we can grow into the fully alive, compassionate and selfless beings we really can be. The essence of each of the principles can fill the voids created within us by modern afflictions such as low self-esteem, loneliness and a sense of alienation. The seven principles of the lion bring us closer to the spirit of the earth, closer to our true selves and closer to true spiritual fulfillment. And closer to the earth's spirit, closer to our true selves and to our spiritual fulfillment we will be kinder to the earth, and to ourselves. We can heal the earth.

Women and Men

In this morally evolving world, I feel that women, historically subjugated, will have an increasingly positive influence upon the earth. I see this very clearly with regard to wildlife issues in Africa and beyond.

In the past, women were seldom allowed in the environmental field, deterred from entering the male-dominated realm of animal research and investigation, seemingly on the grounds that "They feel too much" and would overidentify with the animal being studied.[67] But in the last three decades some of the most significant information that we have learned about animals has been gleaned by women. What they gleaned from their studies has influenced us all.

Through Dian Fossey's work we think of the gorilla called Digit and thereby identify and understand the plight of the gorilla. Joy Adamson brought us a new understanding and positive perception of the lion through the story of Elsa, the lioness. The list of women who have created this awareness and influence is long. In the sixties, Rachel Carson, with her powerful book *Silent Spring*,[68] laid the foundation for the green movement, insisting that every part of the earth is interconnected, organic and endangered. Jane Goodall with the chimpanzees, Beirute Galdikas and the orangutans, Joyce Poole, Daphne Sheldrick and Kathy Payne with elephants, and many, many other women worldwide, through empathizing with the animals they study, in turn champion those animals' cause.

The recent beautiful book *Intimate Nature—the Bond between Women and Animals*[69] abundantly illustrates this fact. In the introduction the editors say:

> These writers and researchers, together with those intellectual and religious traditions, began to mend what was broken by a system of careless thought ... What women have brought to the equation is a respect for feeling and empathy as tools to create intimate bonds of connection ... It has been women, primarily, who have spoken out most often against the suffering and pain of animals, and it has mostly been women who have had the courage to admit their love for the other lives around them. As forbidden a concept as it has seemed in scientific scrutiny, love for another species must always be part of that equation.

The women have emerged, but this should not threaten the male. Lion prides are essentially female societies, made up of interrelated lionesses, mothers, aunts, sisters, etc. Elephants are also similar in their herd make-up. But the lion pride is vulnerable without the existence of the pride males. The males create stability, because they are the ones that can keep hyena clans at bay after a kill is made. Having a strong pride male means that other males cannot take over the pride and in turn inflict infanticide upon existing cubs within the pride.

The modern male should not be threatened by the increasingly empowered woman, but needs to acknowledge the sacredness of women. Women, nature's nurturers, reflect the divine earth upon which we stand, Mother Earth. All men were born from women and are obviously biologically a part of that woman, their mother. Men need to identify with that part of themselves. By recognizing this fact, men can begin to identify with Mother Earth. By identifying the earth as female, a mother, men can identify with all of nature around them. Through this, by seeing the earth as being a part of us, men would go a long way toward not harming the earth. With this would come the realization that harming the earth equals self-destruction.

The earth, men, women, the air, water, the animals, everything is one holy one. By recognizing this, we can all find wholeness and with wholeness comes great wonder.

The Reawakening

Increasingly, today we are recognizing and reaffirming our indelible connection with the earth and nature. We are reaching out to touch the earth and all that lives upon her. We are recognizing the sacredness of the earth and the sacredness within each and every one of us. We are learning that by loving the earth, we can love ourselves. We, after so long, are listening again to the wisdom of the drumbeat of our ancestors.

We are at a time of rediscovery. It is a very exciting time. We are, in different ways, reaching out to touch the divine. The old ways were never dead, but were hidden, quietly waiting for the time when we had reached the stage at which we said: "Enough, I will no longer be alone, living by dictates rooted in shallowness and ignorance." The old ways contain such wide wisdom, for they are of nature and of earth. This wisdom is to be found on the rough intricate bark of a tree, in a single grass seed, in the flow of a brook, in the wind beneath an eagle's wings and in a child's smile. It is wide, this wisdom, all-embracing.

The understanding of how we once used to interrelate with nature, the environment and the earth, and for so long—this is beginning to return today. The sun still rises and it still sets; on cloudless days, the sky is still blue and the tides advance, then ebb as they have always done. Such phenomena, such miracles are the inspiration upon which we should build our connection with the earth. We should do it in the miracle of every breath that we breathe.

The earth speaks to us. It always has. And now, as we did before, we should listen to the earth. To listen is to begin to understand.

The reawakening is happening and these words emphasize this realization.

> Contrary to popular belief, primal religions are today reviving in many parts of the world. The superior attitude that spread European civilization over the globe, spurred on by Western Christianity and materialism, has been discredited in the twentieth century. Native faiths—ways scorned, forbidden, almost destroyed—reached their lowest point at the end of the nineteenth century. Their flame was extinguished. But today the disregard for the earth, for community, for spirituality have brought the whole human enterprise into jeopardy. Arising like a phoenix from the ashes, tribal peoples are gathering again in their ceremonial circles, remembering discarded teaching, renewing the ancient ways.[70]

Renewing the ancient ways. By renewing the ancient ways, those who will come after us will look back at the present time and remember it as a portion of human history when, after so much disconnection, mankind began again to listen to the truth, when man across the world began slowly listening to the ancient drumbeat. It will be a time remembered when spiritual strands of connection began to be built all over the world, touching from continent to continent, heart to heart and soul to soul. This time in which we live will be remembered as the "Reawakening."

When a lion calls upon a grassy plain, a bird sings, and within a cat's contented purrs, energy resonates.

Everything lives; we are all energy, a dynamic pulsating energy called life. Understanding this, one cannot but feel a unity with all life, a unity with God. All things live, and knowing this, we know God lives and exists in us and everything around us. To feel this, to know this, brings celebration to our spirit. And it is wonderful to be alive, and to see life within all things.

By knowing such things, we can embark upon life renewed, feeling cleansed, and new lessons and wisdom will come from new life. Together we can go forward ... To walk with lions.

A Final Word

Remarkably, just as this book was about to be printed, I was told an incredible story that seems to be linked to the healing powers of the lion. Two days ago, I attended an event to raise funds for a haven for adults with cerebral palsy. I was just about to deliver a presentation about my life with lions when a lady came up to me with a copy of my first book, *Cry for the Lions*. She told me that she would dearly like me to sign it and then explained why the book was so important to her.

She told me that around the time that the book was first published in the 1980s, her son was involved in an accident that left him in a coma. For days her son lay in the hospital where he was read to and spoken to in an attempt to elicit a response from him. But this was to no avail. The lady then began reading her son stories about the Tuli lions from *Cry for the Lions*. His condition improved remarkably—and then he came out of the coma. The lady told me that the very first words her son had uttered when he awoke were, "What happened to the lions?"

This remarkable story is, I believe, an affirmation of the healing that is possible to be drawn from the lion. I also believe that I heard this story when I did for an important reason—and that is for it to be told in this book.

Further Information

Gareth conducts lectures and presentations of his life with lions, which include many of the aspects of this book. For more information about these presentations, please contact:

Bookings and Website Management
P.O. Box 345
Blackwood, NJ 08012
USA

Phone: (856) 232 0585
Fax: (856) 228 4128
E-mail: lionmanofafrica@home.com
Visit Gareth's life, lions and work at
www.garethpatterson.com

Suggested Reading
and Viewing

Suggested Reading

George Adamson, *Bwana Game* (Collins & Harvill Press, 1965)

——. *My Pride and Joy* (Collins & Harvill Press, 1986)

Joy Adamson, *Born Free* (Collins & Harvill Press, 1960)

——. *Forever Free* (Collins & Harvill Press, 1962)

——. *Living Free* (Collins & Harvill Press, 1961)

Anthony Bourke and John Rendall, *A Lion Called Christian* (Collins, 1971)

D. J. Conway, *The Mysterious, Magickal Cat* (Llewellyn Publications, 1998)

C. A. W. Guggisberg, *Simba, The Life of the Lion* (Howard Timmins, 1961)

Brain Jackman, *Roaring at the Dawn* (Swan Hill Press, 1995)

Brian Jackman and Jonathan Scott, *The Marsh Lions* (Elm Tree Books, 1982)

Derek and Beverly Joubert, *Hunting with the Moon* (National Geographic Society, 1997)

Kobie Kruger, *All Things Wild and Wonderful* (Penguin, 1997)

Chris McBride, *The White Lions of Timbavati* (Paddington Press, 1977)

Mark and Delia Owens, *Cry of the Kalahari* (Collins, 1984)

Gareth Patterson, *Cry for the Lions* (Frandsen, 1988)

———. *Last of the Free* (Hodder & Stoughton, 1995)

———. *The Lions' Legacy* (Robson Books, 1991)

———. *Making a Killing* (The Captive Animals Society, 2000)

———. *Where the Lions Walked* (Viking, 1991)

———. *With My Soul amongst Lions* (Hodder & Stoughton, 1995)

Judith Rudnai, *The Social Life of the Lion* (The Garden City Press, 1973)

George Schaller, *Golden Shadows, Flying Hooves* (Collins, 1974)

———. *Serengeti: A Kingdom of Predators* (Collins, 1973)

———. *The Serengeti Lion* (University of Chicago Press, 1972)

Lee Server, *Lions* (Todtri Book Publishers, 1999)

Suggested Viewing

Adamson of Africa—Lord of Lions (Yorkshire TV)

The Big Cat Diary (BBC TV)

Born to be Free (see the author's website for details)

Eternal Enemies: Lions and Hyenas (Wildlife Films Botswana)

Lions of Darkness (Wildlife Films Botswana)

The Lions Are Free (Born Free Foundation)

Shadows of Gold and Gray (see the author's website for details)

End Notes

1. David Maybury-Lewis, *Millennium: Tribal Wisdom and the Modern World* (Viking, 1992).

2. Vivienne de Watteville, *Speak to the Earth: Wanderings and Reflections among Elephants and Mountains* (Methuen, 1935; second edition 1986).

3. Quoted by David Maybury-Lewis in *Millennium* (Viking, 1992).

4. Joy Adamson, *Pippa's Challenge* (Collins & Harvill Press, 1972).

5. Paul Harrison, *The Elements of Pantheism: Understanding the Divinity in Nature and the Universe* (Element Books, 1999).

6. Anita Gordon and David Suzuki, *It's a Matter of Survival* (HarperCollins, 1991).

7. Naomi Ozaniec, *The Elements of Egyptian Wisdom* (Element Books, 1994).

8. Sue Carpenter, *Past Lives: True Stories of Reincarnation* (Virgin, 1995).

9. James Serpell, *In the Company of Animals* (Basil Blackwell, 1983).

10. Genesis 1: 28.

11. Genesis 9: 2.

12. Roderick Nash, *Wilderness and the American Mind* (Yale University Press, 1982).

13. Quoted by David Maybury-Lewis in *Millennium* (Viking, 1992).

14. Malidoma Patrice Somé, *The Healing Wisdom of Africa* (Thorsons, 1999).

15. Vivienne de Watteville, *Speak to the Earth* (Methuen 1935; second edition 1986).

16. *Bwana Game. The Life Story of George Adamson* (Collins & Harvill Press, 1968).

17. *Born Free. A Lioness in Two Worlds* (Collins & Harvill Press, 1960).

18. *Where the Lion Walked: The Story of a Journey into the Vanishing Wilderness of the Lion in Contemporary Africa* (Viking, 1991).

19. *Cry for the Lions: A Story of the Lions of Mashatu Epitomizing the Need for the Conservation of the Lions of All Africa* (Frandsen Publishers, South Africa, 1988).

20. Generally, big cat specialists at that time, somewhat short-sightedly, did not regard the lion as endangered. Today, it is estimated that only between ten thousand and thirty thousand lions still grace the African continent, an area three times the size of Europe or China.

21. *The Lions' Legacy* (Robson Books, 1991).

22. *Last of the Free* (Hodder & Stoughton, 1994); *With My Soul Amongst Lions: A Moving Story of the Struggle to Protect the Last Adamson Lions* (Hodder & Stoughton, 1995).

23. *The Cook Report* broadcast its program on canned lion hunting to an audience of some ten million viewers in May 1997.

24. *Dying to be Free: The Canned Lion Scandal and the Case for Ending Trophy Hunting in Africa* (Penguin Books, South Africa, 1998).

25. Giordano Bruno, *Cause, Principle and Unity*, ed. Richard Blackwell (Cambridge University Press, 1998).

26. D. J. Conway, *The Mysterious, Magickal Cat* (Llewellyn Publications, St. Paul, Minnesota, 1998).

27. Tim Stoffel, "The Lion of Judah and the King of Pride Rock" (reproduced on his website www.lionlmb.org/lion).

28. John S. Mbiti, *African Religions and Philosophy* (Heinemann Educational Books, 1969).

29. C. A. W. Guggisberg, *Simba, the Life of the Lion* (Howard Timmins, 1961).

30. Interestingly, female cats are known as "Queens"!

31. George Hunt Williamson, *Secret Places of the Lion* (Spearman, 1958).

32. Robert Bauval, Graham Hancock, *Keeper of Genesis: A Quest for the Hidden Legacy of Mankind* (Heinemann, 1996).

33. The powerful Kingdom of Kush conquered Egypt in 730 BC, ruling for approximately sixty years. This period of Egyptian history is known as the Ethiopian Dynasty.

34. Murry Hope, *Ancient Egypt: the Sirius Connection* (Element Books, 1990).

35. Credo Mutwa, *Isilwane—Tales and Fables* (Struik Publishers Pry Ltd, 1996).

36. Credo Mutwa, *Song of the Stars—The Lore of a Zulu Shaman* (Station Hill, Barrytown Ltd, 1996).

37. Gerhard Lindblom, *The Akamba in British East Africa* (Uppsala University Press, 1920).

38. William Charles Baldwin, *African Hunting, from Natal to Zambesi: including Lake Ngami, the Kalahari Desert, & c. From 1852 to 1860* (R. Bentley, 1863).

39. Sir Alfred Edward Pease, Bt., *The Book of the Lion* (John Murray, 1913).

40. Lee Server, *Lions: A Portrait of the Animal World* (Todtri Book Publishers, New York, 1999).

41. Graham Hancock and Santha Faiia, *Heaven's Mirror—Quest for the Lost Civilization* (Michael Joseph, 1998).

42. Kenneth Clark, *Animals and Men: Their Relationship as Reflected in Western Art from Prehistory to the Present Day* (Thames and Hudson, 1977).

43. Alan F. Alford, *The Phoenix Solution: The Secrets of a Lost Civilization* (Hodder & Stoughton, 1998).

44. Copied by Muazzez Cig of the Istanbul Museum. Translated by Samuel Noah Kramer in *History Begins at Sumer* (Thames and Hudson, 1958).

45. Owen Burnham, *African Wisdom* (Piatkus, 2000).

46. This story was originally told by Michael Main in *Kalahari: Life's Variety in Dune and Delta* (Southern Book Publishers, Johannesburg, 1987).

47. Barry Lopez, *Of Wolves and Men* (Dent, 1978).

48. Evelyn Ames, *A Glimpse of Eden* (Collins, 1968).

49. Credo Mutwa, *Isilwane—Tales and Fables of Africa* (Struik Publishers Pty Ltd, 1996).

50. Sue Carpenter, *Past Lives: True Stories of Reincarnation* (Virgin, 1995).

51. S. A. Thorpe, *African Traditional Religions* (University of South Africa, 1991).

52. Malidoma Patrice Somé, *The Healing Wisdom of Africa* (Thorsons, 1999).

53. It has been proved that the companionship of pets produces healing for humans, and recent studies have shown that they reduce stress-related increases in blood pressure. By simply stroking a cat, for example, the heart rate appears to lower. Pets have even been shown to have the ability to pull individuals out of a severe depression after major trauma.

54. Brian Jackman, *Roaring at the Dawn—Journeys in Wild Africa* (Swan Hill Press, 1995).

55. Vivienne de Watteville, *Speak to the Earth* (Methuen, 1935; second edition 1986).

56. George Adamson, *My Pride and Joy* (Collins & Harvill Press, 1986).

57. Kgosi—Setswana word meaning "chief."

58. In general, lions have a tenure of two to four years as pride males.

59. George Schaller, *Golden Shadows, Flying Hooves* (Collins, 1974).

60. Jeffrey Masson and Susan McCarthy, *When Elephants Weep—the Emotional Lives of Animals* (Jonathan Cape, 1994).

61. Mark and Delia Owens, *Cry of the Kalahari* (William Collins, 1985).

62. Kula the cub's story is told in full in Joy Adamson's book *Queen of Shaba* (Collins & Harvill Press, 1980).

63. Sandy Gall, *George Adamson, Lord of the Lions* (Grafton, 1991).

64. Sandy Gall, *George Adamson, Lord of the Lions* (Grafton, 1991).

65. Kate Turkington, *There's More to Life than Surface* (Penguin, 1998).

66. Jeffrey Masson and Susan McCarthy, *When Elephants Weep—The Emotional Lives of Animals* (Jonathan Cape, 1994).

67. It is no coincidence that for centuries the priesthood, science and almost all positions of power have been held by men.

68. Rachel Carson, *Silent Spring* (Penguin, 1965).

69. Linda Flogan, Deena Metzger, and Brenda Peterson, eds., *Intimate Nature—The Bond between Women and Animals* (Fawcett Columbine, New York, 1998).

70. J. W. E. Newbery, *The World's Religions* (Lion Publishing, 1982).

Other Seastone/Ulysses Press Titles

CHAKRA POWER BEADS: TAPPING THE POWER OF ENERGY
STONES TO UNLOCK YOUR INNER POTENTIAL
Brenda Davies, $9.95
Explains how to improve health, spirit and fortune by fully harnessing the power of beads.

EINSTEIN AND BUDDHA: THE PARALLEL SAYINGS
Thomas J. McFarlane, $19.00
Provocative and insightful, this book demonstrates the parallels between Western thought and Eastern religion and what they communicate about the deep common ground of scientific and spiritual truth.

HOW MEDITATION HEALS: A SCIENTIFIC EXPLANATION
Eric Harrison, $12.95
In straightforward, practical terms, *How Meditation Heals* reveals how and why meditation improves the natural functioning of the human body.

HOW TO MEDITATE: AN ILLUSTRATED GUIDE
TO CALMING THE MIND AND RELAXING THE BODY
Paul Roland, $16.95
Offers a friendly, illustrated approach to calming the mind and raising consciousness through various techniques, including basic meditation, visualization, body scanning for tension, affirmations and mantras.

THE JOSEPH H. PILATES METHOD AT HOME:
A BALANCE, SHAPE, STRENGTH & FITNESS PROGRAM
Eleanor McKenzie, $16.95
This handbook describes and details Pilates, a mental and physical program that combines elements of yoga and classical dance.

KNOW YOUR BODY: THE ATLAS OF ANATOMY
2nd edition, Introduction by Emmet B. Keeffe, M.D., $14.95
Provides a comprehensive, full-color guide to the human body.

PILATES WORKBOOK: ILLUSTRATED STEP-BY-STEP GUIDE
TO MATWORK TECHNIQUES
Michael King, $12.95
Illustrates the core matwork movements exactly as Joseph Pilates intended them to be performed; readers learn each movement by simply following the photographic sequences and explanatory captions.

SENSES WIDE OPEN:
THE ART AND PRACTICE OF LIVING IN YOUR BODY
Johanna Putnoi, $14.95
Through simple, accessible exercises, this book shows how to be
at ease with yourself and experience genuine pleasure in your
physical connection to others and the world.

THE 7 HEALING CHAKRAS:
UNLOCKING YOUR BODY'S ENERGY CENTERS
Brenda Davies, $14.95
Explores the essence of chakras, vortices of energy that connect
the physical body with the spiritual.

SIMPLY RELAX: AN ILLUSTRATED GUIDE
TO SLOWING DOWN AND ENJOYING LIFE
Dr. Sarah Brewer, $15.95
In a beautifully illustrated format, this book clearly presents
physical and mental disciplines that show readers how to relax.

TEACH YOURSELF TO MEDITATE: DISCOVER RELAXATION AND
CLARITY OF MIND IN JUST MINUTES A DAY
Eric Harrison, $12.95
Guides the reader through ten easy-to-follow core meditations.
Also included are practical and enjoyable "spot meditations" that
require only a few minutes a day and can be incorporated into
the busiest of schedules.

WHAT WOULD BUDDHA DO?:
101 ANSWERS TO LIFE'S DAILY DILEMMAS
Franz Metcalf, $15.00
Much as the "WWJD?" books help Christians live better lives by
drawing on the wisdom of Jesus, this "WWBD?" book provides
advice on improving your life by following the wisdom of
another great teacher—Buddha.

WHAT WOULD BUDDHA DO AT WORK?:
101 ANSWERS TO WORKPLACE DILEMMAS
Franz Metcalf and BJ Gallagher Hateley, $16.95
What Would Buddha Do at Work? uses the gentle teachings of
Buddha to help people discover deeper meaning in their work
lives.

*To order these books call 800-377-2542 or 510-601-8301, fax 510-601-
8307, e-mail ulysses@ulyssespress.com, or write to Ulysses Press, P.O.
Box 3440, Berkeley, CA 94703. All retail orders are shipped free of
charge. California residents must include sales tax. Allow two to three
weeks for delivery.*

About the Author

Born in Britain but raised in Africa, Gareth Patterson has worked with lions in wildlife reserves in Botswana, Kenya and South Africa. He inherited the mantle of the "Lion Man of Africa" from George Adamson when, following Adamson's tragic death in 1989, he helped to save three of Adamson's orphan cubs, which he rehabilitated back to the wild. Over the years, Gareth has been involved in many different wildlife projects and campaigns. He has studied lions in the wild, promoted the need for indigenous environmentalism, investigated and exposed the sordid practice of "canned" lion hunting in South Africa, and co-founded of the "Lion Haven," Africa's first natural habitat sanctuary for orphaned lions.